Contents

Internet for the
Retail Travel Industry

Join us on the web at
hospitality-tourism.delmar.com

Internet for the Retail Travel Industry

Ed Maurer

THOMSON
™
DELMAR LEARNING

Australia   Canada   Mexico   Singapore   Spain   United Kingdom   United States

THOMSON
DELMAR LEARNING

Internet for the Retail Travel Industry
Ed Maurer

Business Unit Executive Director:
Susan L. Simpfenderfer

Executive Production Manager:
Wendy A. Troeger

Executive Marketing Manager:
Donna J. Lewis

Executive Editor:
Marlene McHugh Pratt

Production Manager:
Carolyn Miller

Channel Manager:
Wendy Mapstone

Senior Acquisitions Editor:
Joan M. Gill

Production Editor:
Betty L. Dickson

Cover Image:
Gennady Kurbat/© 2002 Brand X Pictures

Editorial Assistant:
Lisa Flatley

For permission to use material from this text or product, contact us by
Tel   (800) 730-2214
Fax   (800) 730-2215
www.thomsonrights.com

Library of Congress Cataloging-in-Publication Data
Maurer, Ed
    Internet for the retail travel industry / Ed Maurer.
        p. cm.
    ISBN 0-7668-4071-9
        1. Travel—Computer network resources.
    2. Internet. 3. World Wide Web. I. Title.

G155.A1 M383 2002
910'.285'4678—dc21

                            2002025612

NOTICE TO THE READER

Chapter 6   **Disseminating Information:
Selling on the Web**   **75**

Chapter 7   **The Web Coordinator: Creating, Updating,
and Monitoring a Web Site**   **85**

Preface

We continue to be bombarded almost daily with stories about the Internet's impact on the way we offer, sell, and book travel services. These tales provide ample evidence that the public at large is increasingly using the Internet for travel information and services. Travel agents have a simple choice: They can ride this wave or be overwhelmed by it. New entrants into the industry do not have a choice: They need travel, computer, and online skills to succeed.

In the background of the matters covered by this text are the following facts:

- Good computers are now available for less than $1,000
- Fiber-optic cabling and other technologies are bringing broadband relief to Internet users who have been frustrated by slow modems
- Resistance to online shopping is crumbling
- Some of the big online travel agencies moved up into the ranks of the 50 largest volume producers in the United States
- High school and college graduates are leaving school computer- and cyber-literate

The new reality of pervasive online computing challenges the way retail agencies and other tourism enterprises do business, and it consequently challenges the way travel is taught. Travel managements and faculties must deal with the fact that the Internet is now part and parcel of our culture and the travel and tourism industries. Students ought to make sure that their travel department's faculty and their prospective employer's management have their focus on a future where the Internet is an integral part of the business and learning environment.

This text introduces students to the online world as it reviews the skills needed to make it in tomorrow's vastly different travel industry. It is hoped that this book will create an awareness and curiosity about the Internet that put students onto a road of continuing education and training.

Acknowledgments

My biggest thanks go to my wife, Helen, without whose moral and editing help this book would never have seen the light of day; and to Stephen Gatlin, for taking a chance on my coming through with this project.

I also thank the travel professionals who read and commented on sections of the book, especially Stephen Kramer of Travel Mart in Mission Viejo; Eric Buehlmann of Switzerland Tourism in Los Angeles; and Shannon M. Risk, Collections Curator at the American Airlines C.R. Smith Museum in Dallas, for the information on the genesis of SABRE.

Last but not least I want to thank the staffs at Amadeus, Galileo International, SABRE Group, and Worldspan for supplying information about their computer reservation systems.

Delmar Learning and the author would like to thank the reviewers who gave of their time and content expertise:

John C. Kesler, Ph.D.
Lakeland Community College
Kirtland, Ohio

Zongquig Zhou, Ph.D.
Niagara University
Buffalo, New York

The author and Delmar Learning affirm that the Web site URLs referenced herein were accurate at the time of printing. However, because of the fluid nature of the Internet, we cannot guarantee their accuracy for the life of the edition.

About the Author

Ed Maurer lives in Mission Viejo, California, just south of the Irvine hotbed of cutting-edge technology parks. He spent many years in the travel industry on both sides of the Atlantic consulting, teaching, web mastering, and writing for the travel and tourism industries. He is now a reference librarian.

Courtesy of the City of
Fullerton, California

CHAPTER 1

Historical Perspective

Chapter Outline

Objectives

After completing this chapter, you should be able to:

- Discuss the origins of the electronic computer and the Internet
- Discuss the evolution of the airline computer reservation system
- Discuss travel industry applications of the Internet

Introduction

During the past 75 years the travel industry and computer technology became ever more intertwined. This chapter gives an overview of this tumultuous three-quarter century.

1929: Vision and Profit

An excellent article by John Brandt related the inception of the Internet to the innovation and events that ushered in commercial aviation. Brandt pointed out that the "buzz about the ... Internet is that while it may eventually be profitable, it still lacks any effective way for mainstream businesses to be profitable [or] to use it in marketing or managing." Brandt reminded these critics that the first commercial coast-to-coast flight in the United States "involved nearly as many miles on the ground as it did time in the air," and that "despite charging an exorbitant price of sixteen cents per mile, Transcontinental Air Transport lost $2.75 million in its first eighteen months." Brandt's trenchant conclusion—still noteworthy even after the dotcom boom and bust of the late 1990s and early 2000s—was that "only a fool judges the commercial future of a technological advance by his own limited vision of the present."[1]

1940s: ENIAC and Vacuum Tubes

In the beginning, there were big, slow, solitary computers. An early behemoth was the Electronic Numerical Integrator and Calculator (ENIAC), the invention of which was driven primarily by the needs of the American defense effort during World War II. This gym-sized, 30-ton machine depended on 17,000 vacuum tubes. Its major problem was not the two technicians needed to check and replace burnt-out tubes or its cumbersome diet of punched cards, but the difficulty of changing programs: applications designed by programmers were literally hardwired into the machine. The unwieldy ENIAC lumbered out to pasture in 1955. Some of its parts can be seen in a Boston museum,[2] where a contemporary sign on one of these ancient, cabinet-sized modules says it all: "In less than forty years, advances in micro-electronics technology have enabled the digital computer with performance far superior to the ENIAC to be placed on a one-quarter-inch piece of silicon."[3] The trend toward miniaturization was set in motion with the invention of the transistor in 1947.

■ 1950s: UNIVAC and Mainframes

Civilian computing started with the installation of a Universal Automatic Computer (UNIVAC) at the U.S. Bureau of the Census, where the machine crunched numbers for population surveys. This machine received its input via magnetic tape rather than by the punch cards that were ENIAC's fibrous diet. Large corporations appreciated the abilities of these new machines, and by the end of the decade, about one thousand UNIVACs were humming at large companies and government departments.[4]

■ 1960s: Jets and SABRE, the First CRS

Nevertheless, computing had certainly not yet made its way into aviation. During the later years of the Eisenhower presidency (1952–1960), many air travelers were still flying aboard propeller planes such as the Douglass DC-6, with a capacity of about 70 passengers. The commercial jet age was ushered in by the British Overseas Airlines Corporation (BOAC) when it inaugurated regular flights with a Comet 4 jet between London and New York on October 4, 1958. Three weeks later, Pan American followed suit, with Boeing 707 jets providing daily flights between New York and Paris, and domestic jet transportation was initiated by National Airlines with flights between New York and Miami in December of that same year. The 707 carried about 180 passengers, about three times the capacity of a DC-6. As of October 1998, the producer of the 707, Seattle-based Boeing Corporation, had ruled most of the civilian skies for 50 years.

At the beginning of the jet age, air transportation was a government-regulated industry. The Civil Aeronautics Board (CAB) controlled fares, and fewer than 1.5 million passengers flew to international destinations.[5] In contrast, in 1995 the airline industry reported almost 500 million domestic boardings and more than 1.2 billion worldwide.[6] Travel agents booked flights over the telephone and wrote tickets by hand. The voluminous *Official Airline Guide (OAG)* appeared monthly with information about fares and schedules.

The appearance of better, cheaper, and faster hardware and software led to major advances in computing. In 1959, the Bank of America revolutionized check processing by introducing magnetic encoding; in 1963, American Airlines introduced the first online computer reservation system (CRS) with its Semi-Automated Business Reservation Environment (SABRE), which used an IBM mainframe computer. By 1964, this system within American Airlines had expanded to reach from coast to coast and from Canada to Mexico. SABRE was the largest computer network outside the U.S. government.

Nevertheless, the defense industry continued to be the driving force in computer design throughout the Cold War years. Much of the government's research money flowed through the Advanced Research Projects Agency (ARPA), the incubator of the Internet. "It started in 1969 as the ARPANET, a network sponsored by the Department of Defense linking computers at university research facilities. It was launched with an exchange of messages between UCLA and the Stanford Research Institute in Menlo Park."[7] The archaic monochrome text-only format of these early exchanges still flickers on some CRS screens.

■ 1970s: Deregulation and Mini-Computers

The first travel agencies hooked up to Apollo (the CRS of United Airlines) and SABRE in 1976; by 1977, American Airlines proudly announced that it had 300 agencies online. CRS services allowed large domestic airlines to sell their tickets cheaply and efficiently through travel agents, and the ease of use of CRSs—along with their income-generating capacities (commissions)—cemented travel agents' dependence on air carriers.

The dominance of large, mainframe computers (mostly manufactured by IBM) was challenged by the introduction of mini-computers. Their design and much smaller size were made possible by the microchip, most notably the TMS 1000 by Texas Instruments. The advent of mini-computers fostered the spread of computer use well beyond Fortune 500 companies to a wider audience, including tour operators and large travel agency chains. As this technology spread, new applications such as word processing also became available. Although mini-computers brought computer technology to a larger public, programmers retained their exclusive status as the only ones able to converse in code with these machines. Programmers' jargon meant job security, just as the coded language needed to use a CRS strengthened the travel industry's monopoly on access to computerized travel information.

Federally mandated domestic airline deregulation began in 1978, and it severely challenged the structure of the airline and retail travel industries. According to an American Airlines press release, "the effects of deregulation are still being felt ... . Whereas in 1977 roughly 37 percent of airline passengers traveled on discounted fares, [in 1993] that number is closer to 92 percent ... . Needless to say, by the late [19]70s, travel agencies needed CRS terminals to handle the growing number of passengers, and SABRE's client base grew by leaps and bounds. In March 1979, we installed SABRE in our 1,000th subscriber location."[8] The number of agencies more than doubled within 10 years of deregulation, the number of airlines more than tripled, and passenger numbers soared even more. This explosion of air travel richly rewarded travel agents with a bonanza of commission income even while many airlines sank into a sea of red accounting ink. As a consequence, airline wages shrank and airline bankruptcies became common. Airline efforts to reduce commissions were bitterly contested and successfully thwarted by travel agents, who maintained their near-monopoly on ticket issuance.

■ 1980s: The Personal Computer

Important inventions of the mid- and late 1970s began to blossom in the next decade. Daniel Bricklin conceived Visicalc (the world's first electronic spreadsheet) while he was a graduate student at Harvard University. "VisiCalc was successful [because it allowed] users to use this electronic spreadsheet to manipulate numbers in a myriad of ways. This was something that couldn't be done on an IBM mainframe."[9] Two California dreamers, Jobs and Wozniak, created the Apple microcomputer in their San Jose garage to run this new software. Businesses began to use it for nimble accounting, budgeting, and forecasting. IBM belatedly entered the microcomputer arena with its benchmark Personal Computer (PC), running on the now-venerable DOS (Disk Operating System) created by Bill Gates and Paul Allen of Microsoft. The PC turned out to be the first computer that users could operate effectively and directly, without the need of a programmer. Soon the PC would also handle database management, graphics, and word processing in addition to spreadsheet applications.

While PCs were becoming ever-better stand-alone business machines, researchers began to use theirs to communicate with each other:

> Sending and receiving messages via the ARPANET became possible and E-Mail as we know it was born along with the by-now universal @ symbol in addresses. When ARPANET enabled incompatible computers to "talk" to each other, many new networks

were created. They soon bypassed the ARPANET and communicated directly with one another: the Internet was born and the ARPANET was decommissioned in 1989.[10]

Just as soon as the Internet appeared, EasySABRE[SM] was created to provide frequent travelers and online computer users with easy-to-use access to the SABRE global distribution system (GDS).

The PC became the king of computer land, replacing the mini-computer almost entirely and relegating the mainframe and its attendant programmers to large-scale tasks. As a result, working with the PC and its growing software library became normal in many sectors of American education, business, and industry. People used the PC and its ever-growing connectivity, speed, and versatility to increase efficiency. The PC's attraction was hugely enhanced with the introduction of Microsoft's Windows operating system, which gave PC users an easy, graphics-oriented way to access applications.

By contrast, retail travel agencies generally missed the PC revolution, and continued to use their PCs primarily as CRS terminals (see Figure 1-1). Why didn't PC use blossom in the travel industry as it did in just about every other sector of American business? Whatever the reasons, the lack of computer literacy among travel agents became one of the retail travel industry's major handicaps.

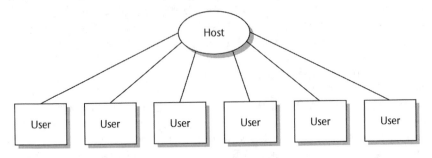

FIGURE 1-1 The hierarchical structure of a CRS computer network

▇ 1990s: Online Communications and Commission Caps

When Tim Berners-Lee invented the World Wide Web in 1990, the PC "went platinum" and the Internet began to move to center stage. Lee's invention made the Internet more user-friendly by adding graphics and the point-and-click capacity to connect almost instantly to just about any file, format, resource, or tool available on the Internet. In a very short time, the Web became the dominant feature of the Internet. Most companies use the Internet and its mind-boggling resources to transact their business, and online home computers connect about a quarter of America's households to cyberspace. By contrast, many travel agencies remain shackled to their CRSs, and their connections to the Internet are tenuous and underused. This lack of modern, online technology and the absence of computer savvy puts many travel agencies at a serious disadvantage in the current business environment.

Companies and organizations have connected to—and established presences on—the Internet at an astonishing pace, and its penetration of U.S. business is widespread. In Orange County, California, an Internet frontier, nine out of ten businesses were online by 1997, according to the *Los Angeles Times*.[11] The same article estimated that private participation in this same area had reached the magic 25 percent mark—magic because at this level of acceptance the new item or service becomes commonplace, and everybody has to have it. Without doubt, the Internet in Orange County has become a standard business, educational, communications, marketing, and research tool.

With decent computers costing less than $1,000, and with popular public access points for the general public proliferating, the Internet became accessible to most people. Libraries, convenience stores, truck stops, and Internet cafes were especially popular with travelers wanting to stay in touch via the Internet.[12] The Cyber Java Cafe of Venice, California, issued this manifesto:

> The profound gains for society offered by the Internet may be unevenly distributed if the large population without knowledge or access to computers are left out of Cyberspace. Promises of a "global village" and "digital democracy" may be unfulfilled if computers remain the exclusive tool of the specially educated or affluent. Cyber Java's mission is to bring Internet education and connectivity to coffee drinkers everywhere!

Many cafes and software programs included the term *Java* to indicate a connection with both the popular beverage and the application program called Java. The application was important for two reasons: It was the first programming language not specific to a particular operating system or microprocessor, and it transformed the Web from a text- and still-picture medium into an animated, more television-like medium. With Java, the brainchild of people at Sun Microsystems, and XML (Extended Markup Language), the Web took the quantum leap from hypertext to hypermedium (see Figure 1-2 on page 8).

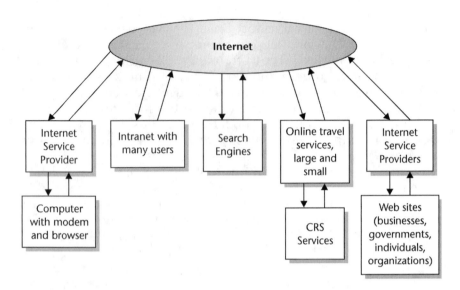

FIGURE 1-2 The structure of the Internet

In 1996, when 36 percent of households in the United States had PCs (in trendy southern California, the percentage was 46[13]), SABRE debuted Travelocity on the World Wide Web. It was the first full-service, online, travel booking and information resource available to users of the Web. This service was squarely aimed at an upscale public, because computer literacy remained a trait of the more educated middle and upper classes: More than 80 percent of students entering private colleges used computers regularly.[14] However, only 22 percent of southern California households with incomes of less than $25,000 had personal computers, compared with 69 percent of those with incomes of more than $50,000. The most technologically adept were overwhelmingly male and highly educated.[15] By contrast, the typical full-time travel agent was female, with a high school diploma, earning less than $20,000 annually.[16] These figures may explain why computer and cyber-literacy were below average in the retail travel industry.

The winter of 1995 marked the introduction of commission caps. Since then, commissions paid by many airlines to travel agents have been reduced to zero. The sale of domestic air transportation in particular became less lucrative for travel agents. Airlines were chary with commissions, and started to promote ticketless travel, special Web sites for frequent travelers, and auctions—three techniques that helped to increase direct sales. Therefore, agents with their ears to the ground and a feel for the industry started to automate ticket sales and began to shift their agents' emphasis from the sale of airline tickets to high-margin cruises, packages, and tours. Home-based agents, niche marketing, and specialization found increasing favor as ways to remain profitable.

Millions of surfers used large, sophisticated Web sites, such as Expedia, Preview Travel, and Travelocity, for their travel needs, and some airlines offered complete travel services on their Web sites. Overall, the volume of travel services booked over the Internet almost quadrupled from 1996 to 1997, yet travel agents' share of this rapidly growing pie shrank from 79 percent to 52 percent during the same period. Another indication of what the future might bring was supplied by the Travel Industry Association of America, which estimated that online bookings for air travel, hotels, car rentals, and other travel products would grow from $827 million in 1997 to nearly $9 billion by 2002.

■ 2000s: Evolution of the CRS

Actions taken by the Federal Communications Commission in early April of 1997 were intended to enable 50 percent of the American public to watch digital television (HDTV) by Christmas 1999. This new broadcast signal blurs the distinction between a computer and a TV. This convergence almost guaranteed that the Internet would reach critical mass in the United States by the year 2000, when 25 percent of the U.S. population was estimated to have gone online. From this threshold of acceptance, the Internet changed from something optional to something required.

The growth of the Internet was predicted to be even faster by Kate Delhagen, an analyst with Forrester's People & Technology Strategies service: "[B]y 2001, 135 million people in the United States will be communicating through e-mail. In other words, e-mail will reach 50 percent of the U.S. population within five years. Growth will be fueled by the increase in home PC penetration and business to business online transactions."[17] By 1998, the volume of e-mail exceeded the volume of letters sent by regular postal mail.

Many consumers have used, and will continue to use, their point-and-click personal computer or television appliance to access information and to transact business. This trend holds great promise for the travel industry, but dangers lurk in this brave new world. Just as telephone directory assistance and retail banking (think automated teller machines) are now carried out mostly by machines, airline reservations will become almost totally automated. The *New York Times* noted that "the airline industry is trying to persuade frequent flyers to book their own flights with software that takes advantage of point-and-click technology and offers more sophisticated features than EasySABRE."[18] Even if the public wants to keep making reservations with live travel agents, the cost savings for airlines and CRSs will drive automation to the furthest possible extent.

The Internet's Janus-faced nature will manifest itself dramatically in the travel industry: On the one hand, the Internet will eliminate dealing with air reservations as a major part of an agent's job description; on the other hand, it will create tools for travel design, marketing, and research of an efficiency and quality unimaginable just a few years ago. The power of the Internet will shift travel agents' focus from being reservations and ticketing processors to being travel consultants dealing in the complex products that online services do not handle well (see Figure 1-3).

According to an associate of Cruise Shoppes America (CSA), Robin's Travel Service in Lake Worth, Florida, "those who are not sold on the Internet are wasting money, time and sales." An associate explained:

> Clients came into our agency wanting to go to the Oktoberfest in Germany. They wanted to know when it would take place and what events were happening. We could have written the German

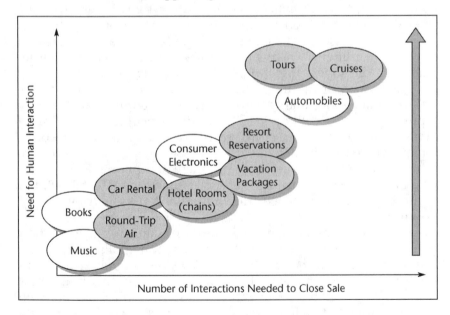

FIGURE 1-3 Complex products require customer support to close the sale

Consulate and waited a month for the information and lost the sale, but it's all right there on the Internet—dates, events, even a listing of all the different beer tents. We were able to provide our clients all the information they needed in less than 10 minutes.[19]

Is it any wonder that organizations such as the German National Tourist Board are closing offices while expanding their Web sites?

■ Summary

Personal computers and online communication have become common in many sectors of American life and business. Although a late bloomer, the retail travel industry is beginning to adapt to this new reality. As this adaptation spreads, the power and capabilities of the Internet will shift travel agents' focus from being reservations and ticketing processors to being travel consultants, sales, and marketing experts.

End Notes

[1] John Brandt, "Naysayers Need a History Lesson," *Industry Week,* 5 June 1995, 6.

[2] The Computer Museum in Boston charts the history of the computer from the vacuum-tube era to Web TV and beyond.

[3] Philip Elmer-DeWitt, "A Birthday Party for ENIAC," *Time,* 24 February 1986, 63.

[4] Linda Runyan, "Forty Years on the Frontier," *Datamation,* 15 March 1991, 34.

[5] U.S. Bureau of the Census, *Statistical Abstract of the United States* (Washington, D.C.: Government Printing Office, 1961), 198.

[6] Aerospace Industries Association of America, *Aerospace Facts & Figures 1995–96* (Washington, D.C.: Author).

[7] Amy Harmon, "Computing in the '90s: 'The Great Divide,' " *Los Angeles Times,* 7 October 1996, D1–D6.

[8] American Airlines press release, 1 March 1993.

[9] Runyan, "Forty Years on the Frontier," 34.

[10] *Los Angeles Times Magazine,* 27 October 1996, 9.

[11] Jonathan Weber, "Download This: The Dirty Secret about the Net—Hint: It's About Money (But Isn't It Always?)," *Los Angeles Times* (home ed.), 21 February 1997, D1–D6.

[12] Margaret Webb, *Washington Post,* 1 August 1995, D1.

[13] Greg Miller, "Getting with the PC Program," *Los Angeles Times,* 6 October 1996, 1, 36.

[14] William H. Honan, "College Freshmen's Internet Use a Way of Life, but Disparities Emerge," *New York Times on the Web*, 25 January 1999. Retrieved March 7, 2000 from **http://www.nytimes.com**.

[15] Harmon, "Computing in the '90s," D6.

[16] U.S. government figures for 1994 showed these annual incomes for travel agents: median $21,300; less than 1 year experience, $12,990; 1–3 years' experience, $16,481; 3–5 years' experience, $19,491; 5–10 years' experience, $22,122; more than 10 years' experience, $24,645. U.S. Department of Labor, Bureau of Labor Statistics, *Occupational Outlook Handbook* (Washington, D.C.: Government Printing Office, 1997).

[17] *ISP World*, 3 March 1997, 20.

[18] David K. Johnston, "Practical Traveler: Do It Yourself," *New York Times*, 30 June 1996, section 5, 4.

[19] Paid advertisement in *TravelTrade Magazine*, 24 March 1994.

CHAPTER 2

Travel Reservations and the Internet

Chapter Outline

Objectives
After completing this chapter, you should be able to:
- Discuss the potential of the Internet for the retail travel industry and for consumers
- Identify new online competitors
- Compare the major computer reservations systems

■ The End of Exclusivity and Monopolies

Travel agents had an almost exclusive lock on travel knowledge before the advent of the Internet: They had sole access to up-to-date transportation information, and they had the voluminous documentation needed to make intelligent travel decisions (hotel guides, cruise and visa information, and so on). What's more, through CRS access, airlines gave travel agents a virtual monopoly to provide the public—conveniently and quickly—with travel documents and information (reservations, schedules, tickets, and the like). However, economic and technological changes eroded much of this monopoly. Airlines reduced the need for paper tickets, and reduced or entirely eliminated travel agent commissions. Non-travel-industry entities, such as Ticketmaster, began offering travel services, and the Internet enabled anyone with a personal computer to access CRS and other travel services. The Internet brought profound changes to the travel and transportation industries in part because of this individual access opportunity and in part because it offered cost reductions and low-cost marketing and sales opportunities. These were advantages no industry could safely ignore.

Automation

Many travel agencies began to install computer terminals in the 1970s, long before the personal computer became commonplace in other small businesses. Airlines granted travel agencies CRS access, allowing them to gather information and to process reservations more efficiently. The CRS was created at a time when all such systems were hierarchical and separate: Each large airline made decisions and its client or subscriber agencies followed instructions. Looked at another way, the CRS organization was set up much like a walled, medieval city-state with a defined ruling class (airline management) making the important business and governmental decisions—sometimes in a high-handed fashion, but always ostensibly for the good of the common people (the travel agent community).

In contrast, the Internet's organization (or lack thereof) is much like that of modern Los Angeles: an open city without a clearly defined or dominant center. The individual energy of its inhabitants let business centers sprout up willy-nilly, responding to local needs and whims, without much attention to overall planning or the common good.

The Personal Computer

While the majority of travel agencies depended on CRS-supplied hardware and software as their major business tool, other businesses and industries adopted the stand-alone personal computer as their workhorse. Many of these small, independent computer users connected to the Internet, where they freely communicated with each other in an open, nonhierarchical environment. The importance of this development cannot be overstated. The culture of the Internet was something entirely new, challenging existing business structures, relationships, and values.

▪ The Internet Lured Powerful New Competitors to the Travel Industry

The Internet brought competition and movement to the field of travel service delivery, and it offered opportunities for travel agents—so much opportunity that some online travel services joined the ranks of the top-producing agencies in the country. Jim Frederick of *Money* magazine provided a glimpse of what consumers could do when selecting a provider of travel services. His article also pinpointed what good Internet travel sites at the time looked like, what they offered, and what features they had that were likely to be useful to consumers. After describing the deal that his "wizardlike travel agent" took only 10 minutes to book, Frederick decided to do a little experimentation and comparison shopping. He had heard that the rapidly proliferating Internet

> sites give users access to the same vast and ever-changing reservation databases that travel agents themselves subscribe to. That means you can hunt for the lowest prices yourself, from your own computer, at any hour. So I decided to fire up the old browser to see what the most popular full-service travel agents on the Web could do for me.
>
> The results? Well, overall, I'm sorry I strayed. Eight hours, six sites and thousands of mouse clicks later, I had yet to find and book a complete package to match [my travel agent's]. Still, I did turn up enough compelling information to convince me that, under some circumstances, these sites can be useful tools.[1]

After two weeks of experimentation with various trip combinations, Frederick concluded that the huge amount of time needed for multiple searches, using complex and sometimes challenging interfaces, weighed heavily against the self-booking option—even though some sites offered lower prices on portions of the package than the travel agent. Nevertheless, he recommended that would-be travelers check around for current offerings and lowest fares so that they would know what to expect from a travel agent.

Frederick also praised three sites in particular. The first was Preview Travel, which has since been acquired by Sabre, Inc., and folded into Travelocity (thus making Travelocity the most visited travel site on the Internet at that time). He particularly liked the site's "best-fare finder"and search-screen capabilities, though he found its hotel booking capacity limited.

Another standout was Microsoft Expedia (**http://www.expedia. msn.com**), which had user-friendly password memory, good fare trackers, and nonstop-flight screening ability. Mr. Frederick was not alone in his regard for this service: Expedia received many awards, and at the close of the year 2000, Ziff-Davis *Smart Business* and *Mobile Computing & Communications, Town and Country,* Yahoo!, and *PC Magazine* rated Expedia the "Best Travel Site of the Year."

Travelocity (**http://www.travelocity.com**) also offered competitive air fares and rates (see Figure 2-1), and allowed criteria ranking to guide its fare searches. However, the site limited the number of itineraries per search, and had a "poorly designed" hotel section.[2]

The sites reviewed in Frederick's article underwent changes thereafter, of course. A notable addition in the summer of 2001 was Orbitz (**http://www.orbitz.com**), an effort by several major airlines to compete with Travelocity, Expedia, and other online travel agencies. Founded by American, Continental, Delta, Northwest, and United Airlines, Orbitz had the money and clout to put a truly competitive product on the market. It offered consumers real-time search capabilities covering 455 airlines in an unbiased environment. Orbitz also boasted that it had the Internet's biggest collection of low-cost, Web-only fares.

■ CRSs and the Internet

As they evolved, online travel services tried to work out the many kinks in procedures that made them a less-than-attractive alternative to travel agents for many travelers. They also tried to connect directly with vendors, such as airlines, hotels, and car rental companies, rather than through the expensive CRS intermediary.

CRS services thus had to offer new services to remain competitive with the likes of America West Airlines, which allowed agents direct access to its reservation system through the Internet, bypassing any CRS intermediary; and with mighty Microsoft, whose

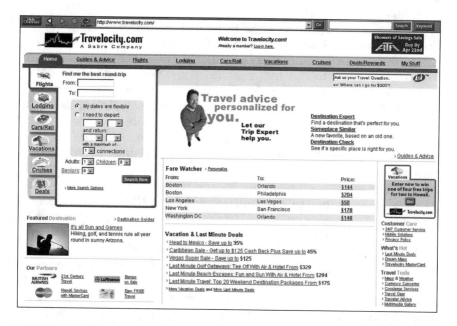

FIGURE 2-1 Home page of Travelocity. ©2002 Travelocity.com L.P. Used
by permission. All rights reserved. Republication or
redistribution is expressly prohibited without the prior
written consent of Travelocity.com L.P.

Expedia online service directly challenged travel agents and the
CRS distribution system. It's no wonder that many new CRS products were all Internet enabled. Inevitably, the distinction between
CRS and Internet became blurred, and the traditional CRS became
part of the Internet universe. *Note:* This book continues to use
the traditional term *CRS* when referring to these information
distribution systems, although the abbreviation *GDS* (for global
distribution system) gained currency quickly.

Convergence

With the advent of the Internet as an alternate or additional
distribution channel for travel services, technology-savvy travel
agents began to use the new medium to increase efficiency and
profitability. Under this strategy, the CRS activity portion of an
agency's business decreases, but the Internet activity increases.
The shift occurred gradually, but it is important to recognize its
implications and potential.

The convergence of CRSs and Internet-based services was
driven by the rapid spread of the Internet, which in turn was

accelerated by continuous reductions in the cost of hardware. Ellie Knight, Director of Technology and Training, Leisure Travel Group in Marina del Rey, California, noted, "There are cheaper solutions to desktop access to the Internet and those provided by the CRSs, which are very limited in scope. A good technician should be able to configure an average travel agency with a simple solution for about $500, according to our research."[3] Computer systems costing less than $1,000, in conjunction with the various CRS dial-up services, allowed travel agents to work from home and to effectively become telecommuters. This reduced the need for agencies to include hardware within their CRS contracts.

The convergence of Internet services and CRS services spelled absorption of or even extinction for some of the latter; given this, it is curious that CRS services encouraged their travel agency subscribers to use the Internet. This apparent contradiction may be explained by the CRS services' desperate need for travel agency business, since they stood to lose volume to companies that dealt directly with vendors (airlines, hotels, car rental companies, and so on). CRS services may continue to try to enlist travel agencies in their fight for domination of travel distribution services against companies that bypass them.

Later developments illustrated the danger the Internet posed to CRS services. Inteletravel, working primarily with outside travel sales representatives (SOHO entrepreneurs), tried to attract travel agents with a system that was purportedly more efficient than traditional CRS platforms. E-Travel, a corporate online travel system, planned to offer its agency and corporate clients access to air, hotel, and car reservations without a CRS intermediary. Online travel booking systems that formerly used CRSs to connect their clients with reservation services began to bypass the CRS services in favor of direct deals between online travel companies (such as E-Travel, Preview Travel, and Microsoft Expedia) and providers (such as Continental Airlines, Hertz Rent-A-Car, and Pegasus Systems, a company connecting many hotels with CRS services).

With big, well-financed online travel companies, CRS services faced adversaries that proved more difficult to handle and cope with than travel agencies were. A profile of a leading online travel service from 1998 is instructive.

Preview Travel, Inc.

According to this San Francisco-based company's own press releases, online travel gross bookings grew to almost $200.1 million in 1998, up 149 percent from 1997. Revenues were $14 million (7 percent of gross sales), up 133 percent compared to 1997. The company also boasted about its rapidly growing advertising, non-air income, and number of subscribers: the latter reached 6.4 million (up 3.8 million) in 1998. Nevertheless, this company, whose stock was traded on NASDAQ under "PTVL," lost $22.1 million in 1997, albeit at a shrinking rate of $2.11 per share versus $3.54 per share the previous year. The development of the share price from 1997 to 1998 suggested great investor confidence, as it rose from $7.56 on December 31, 1997, to $18.44 on December 31, 1998.

The company accepted bookings directly from consumers and had strategic alliances with America Online, Excite, Fodors, Lycos, Mastercard, SNAP!, and *USA Today*. It is noteworthy that the company made efforts to shift business from generally low-fee air bookings to services that generated better revenue, such as car rentals and hotel and vacation packages.

■ CRS Comparisons

The established CRS companies and their travel agents had to learn new tricks to compete with the new online travel services. The following descriptions show how the CRS companies upgraded their services to remain ahead of the curve.

Each CRS tried to take advantage of new technologies differently, and it was difficult to compare their qualities fairly and fully, especially as they continually adapted to their changing marketplaces. Each system released material claiming that it was the biggest and the best. Figure 2-2 on page 20 highlights each system's characteristics relevant to U.S. travel agencies. The four services were those with the greatest market penetration in terms of participating U.S. agency locations. Naturally, the two major systems—Apollo/Galileo and SABRE—get the lion's share of this section.

SABRE

SABRE was a leading provider of technology for the travel industry. This publicly held company provided products that both enabled travel commerce and services and enhanced airline/supplier operations. SABRE owned 70 percent of Travelocity.com, the world's leading online business-to-consumer (B2C) travel site; and GetThere, the world's leading business-to-business (B2B) travel site. The company's revenue in the year 2000 amounted to $2.5 billion.

	Apollo	SABRE	Amadeus	Worldspan
Major Owner(s)	Aer Lingus, Air Canada, Alitalia, Austrian Airlines, British Airways, KLM, Olympic, Swissair, TAP, United, US Airways	AMR	Air France, Iberia, Lufthansa	Delta, Northwest, TWA
Agency Products				
Windows Program	Focalpoint	PlanetSABRE	Amadeus	Worldspan for Windows
Internet Program	Travelpoint	Web Reservations	Amadeuslink	WorldspanGo!
Corporate Travel	Travelpoint	BTS	Corporate Circle	Worldspan Trip Manager
Public Web Site	Travelpoint	Travelocity	Amadeuslink.com	WorldspanGo!

FIGURE 2-2 CRS characteristics compared (as of 1998)

SABRE connected more than 66,000 travel agents around the world, providing content from 450 airlines, 50,000 hotels, 54 car rental firms, 8 cruise lines, 33 railroads, and 228 tour operators. It also included content and connections to large retail travel operations such as American Express Travel, Associated Travel, Carlson Travel Group, Rosenbluth International, Thomas Cook Group, and many others. In its effort to expand beyond the travel industry, SABRE served companies and entities as diverse as AMOCO, ESPN, NationsBank, Pacific Gas & Electric, the Panama Canal Commission, and the U.S. Navy, among others.

SABRE Products for Retail Travel Agents

SABRE presented its continually evolving and expanding products for travel agencies and agents in a multitiered marketing package named SABRE eVoya. It was divided into four components:

desktop, delivery, content, and tools. The entire SABRE product line was expertly presented, and described in detail on SABRE's Web site, http://www.sabre.com/products/index.html.

SABRE Products for Both Travel Agents and Travelers

SABRE's "Virtually There" product allowed agencies to add valuable services to their own Web pages. A "Virtually There" link allowed customers to visit an agency's Web site, click on the appropriate link, and check existing flight itineraries. What's more, agents could share information about existing reservations with clients by inserting appropriate links in e-mails. "Virtually There" added interactivity and credibility to an agency's Web site—enhancements appreciated by clients who were used to sophicated sites like those of Expedia and Travelocity.

Travelocity

A vote of 250,000 travel agents in 83,000 agencies in 141 countries named Travelocity the world's leading Internet travel site. Inaugurated in 1996, it quickly became one of the most powerful one-stop sites on the Internet, with more than 1.5 million members selling more than $1 million worth of travel services on record days. Although Travelocity worked directly with consumers, it also featured a travel agency directory that listed participating SABRE agencies. Consumers could make all their travel arrangements electronically and have travel documents issued by their participating SABRE agent; in other words, reservations made through Travelocity's travel agent directory were routed directly to the agency selected by the consumer. Although participation in this directory was free to all SABRE agencies, they had to activate this Internet option in their travel journal records.

SABRE Web Reservations

Any SABRE agency could quickly establish a presence on the World Wide Web with this companion product to Travelocity. SABRE Web Reservations was for agents only: Consumers visited an agency's Web site—complete with logo, address, contact numbers, and so on—and enjoyed the services of Travelocity under the agency's banner. This was seen as a good way to compete against online giants such as Preview Travel. Although this Web site's reservation capability was free of charge, there were one-time fees for logo branding, usage fees for queued passenger name records (PNRs), and possible transaction excesses.

SABRE Business Travel Solutions

SABRE Business Travel Solutions was a complete travel management solution for corporations and their travel agencies. It allowed individual business travelers to connect to up-to-date travel information sources using their own desktop or laptop computers. This versatile application could be used in corporate intranet, Microsoft Windows, and Lotus Notes environments. Employees could make reservations that met the requirements and guidelines of their corporations' corporate travel policies. The SABRE Business Travel Solutions package featured Agency Link technology, providing seamless integration between corporations and their travel agencies.

SABRE's Technology Strategies

SABRE summarized its view of the future in an extensive statement of technical direction for electronic travel distribution.[4] To move the rapidly increasing amount of information, the SABRE network was to use Frame Relay and TCP/IP at a standard speed of 56Kbps. These enhancements were intended to lead to seamless integration of content from SABRE Agent Explorer and graphics (images, maps, photos) on the Internet.

SABRE positioned itself as an electronic point-of-sales system for very perishable travel services. Figure 2-3 illustrates a travel distribution model with four parts:

1. Buyer data contained in PNRs and other client records
2. Seller data contained in CRS databases
3. Fulfillment loop producing travel documents
4. Transaction kernel where items 1–3 interact

This vision of the future placed the SABRE travel distribution network firmly in the Internet arena.

Galileo International and Apollo Travel Services

In June 2001, Cendant Corporation, which owned Avis car rental and the Days Hotel chain, acquired Galileo International for almost $3 billion in stock and cash. Thus, what started as United Airlines' reservation system evolved into a global distribution system (GDS) owned by a vast conglomerate, where it had to show that it could be as profitable as Avis and Days Inns. This was quite

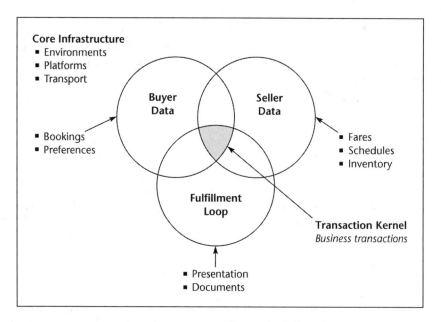

FIGURE 2-3 Travel distribution model (Adapted from
http://www.travel.sabre.com/tech/sotd12.htm)

a challenge, as the GDS business was growing slowly and travel agents—the major source of Galileo's revenue—were retrenching because of narrower margins and competition from online travel sites and companies.

According to David Tongut, a research analyst for Morgan Stanley Dean Witter,[5] "one of the primary differences between Galileo and The SABRE Group is that Galileo tends to be more of a cautious follower when it comes to technology ... . Galileo is much more overseas focused compared to SABRE." This overseas emphasis stemmed from the system's international ownership (Aer Lingus, Air Canada, KLM, Swissair, and United owned about two-thirds of Galileo International). In stark contrast to SABRE's business plan, which called for expansion beyond the travel industry, Galileo International stated that "the company's growth is driven by airline bookings."[6] Galileo International operated two computerized reservation systems: Apollo® was marketed in Canada, the United States, Mexico, Japan, and certain islands in the Caribbean; and the Galileo® system was offered in the rest of the world. Because this book is for use in the United States, we discuss the services of Apollo Travel Services, a fully owned subsidiary of Galileo International.

Apollo Services for Travel Agencies

Galileo International distributed its services to U.S. travel agents through Apollo Travel Services, while retaining its traditional name and image.

Focalpoint

Focalpoint pioneered the integration of Windows-based technology with its CRS back in 1987. Focalpoint 3.0 made the Apollo system responsive to agencies' needs by including several Windows tools for third-party compatibility. Because Focalpoint used the Windows environment, it was easy to operate, "eliminating the need to learn 'computerese.' "[7]

Focalpoint Dial-Up®

The "Dial-Up®" service made Focalpoint fully portable. With the correct passwords, any Internet-connected computer could provide an experienced user with Focalpoint services anywhere. It was great for presentations away from the office, or for access to the CRS during business trips.

Focalpoint Remote Office

The Remote Office capability allowed several agents to connect their home computers, using Focalpoint software that gave them the same interface as at the office. A Focalpoint local area network (LAN) was required at the agency location to run this software.

Focalpoint SE™

Focalpoint SE™ served agencies that wanted to control the selection, purchase, and installation of their hardware. All the features included in Focalpoint 3.0 were packaged with Focalpoint SE™.

Focalpoint Relay™ Productivity Tools

The Relay™ suite of services provided agency automation beyond Focalpoint by increasing productivity for both inexperienced and expert agents. It helped capture data such as itineraries, PNRs, and queues to convert them to other uses such as PRO-files, editing, e-mail, and fax.

Premier™ Car and Hotel Applications

Premier™ was just one of the many applications provided by Apollo Travel Services as a graphical (Windows-based) alternative. These applications enabled novice agents to handle booking cars and hotels immediately through the Apollo® system.

Viewpoint™

Viewpoint™ was Galileo's third attempt to present a graphical user interface (GUI) for use by travel agencies. Viewpoint™ brought the point-and-click environment, so well known to Windows and World Wide Web users, to travel agents. The software could be used by 486 computers and was free of charge. According to a senior vice president of Subscriber Marketing at Galileo International, "Viewpoint help[ed] travel agencies become more customer-focused by allowing them to concentrate on developing their sales and customer service skills instead of spending valuable time learning traditional entry formats."[8]

Galileo International Services for Consumers

Travelpoint In contrast to SABRE, Galileo International opted to channel all online bookings on this site through agents, stating that "Travelpoint.com™ is brought to you by your Apollo® travel agency and Galileo International." However, Galileo was the CRS for public travel sites such as America Online (AOL) and Internet Travel Network (ITN). Travelpoint was an Internet-based booking product that was integrated with the core Apollo and Galileo reservation systems. This online booking engine allowed travelers to make their own air, hotel, and car reservations, with all ticketing done by an Apollo travel agent. Travelpoint was designed to serve both private and corporate travelers and it asked the user to choose between services for the general traveler or for the corporate traveler. Once the user selected the appropriate area of the site, existing corporate travel policies and individual preferences were automatically observed. Users could also view their current and past itineraries and make changes to their personal profiles.

Travel agents were able to personalize their Travelpoint.com Web sites with their own agency's name, address, and logo, and could also customize it for each of their corporate accounts. With this product, agents could compete with industry behemoths such as Preview Travel (now part of Travelocity).

A Galileo International press release touted Travelpoint.com as "a tremendous low-cost opportunity to improve corporate control, traveler convenience and agency productivity. It enables agencies to increase their focus on high value services and provides an option for more effective travel management programs."[9]

Corporate Travelpoint™ Attempting to catch up with SABRE's Business Travel Solutions, Apollo combined forces with Internet Travel Network to create Corporate Travelpoint™. It was designed to meet the most exacting travel management requirements of the largest corporations, by giving corporate travel managers the ability to:

- Rank preferred air, car, and hotel vendors by specific market
- Administer air, car, and hotel contracts to ensure that travelers used preferred vendors
- Enforce corporate policy compliance through exception reporting and approval

Worldspan

On a global basis, Worldspan was the smallest of the major CRS services. Its history dated back to 1968, when an internal reservation system (later named DATAS II®) became operational for Delta Airlines, and to 1971, when a similar system (later named PARS®) was started by Trans World Airlines (TWA). Northwest Airlines became a co-owner of PARS.

In 1990, Delta, Northwest Airlines, and TWA combined their CRS services, and by 1994, the three systems' unification as Worldspan was completed. Ownership of the CRS in 1998 reflected this background: Delta (38 percent), Northwest (32 percent), and TWA (25 percent). World headquarters were in Atlanta, Georgia, and International Division headquarters were in London.

Worldspan's two lines of business were (1) the CRS, serving travel agency and associate customers worldwide; and (2) the airline services operation, providing hosting and related technical services to a growing number of both major and smaller airlines. Because the owners were aware of the declining share of airline ticket distribution by travel agents, they sought new information technology (IT) and CRS business to keep the company profitable.

Worldspan redesigned its services and clustered travel agency services under the title WorldspanGo®. This was a Web-based concept in travel technology that represented high-speed digital access to a worldwide electronic marketplace of travel and travel-related information. It featured:

- Graphical user interfaces for airline, car, and hotel bookings
- A browser-based reservation system
- A real-time preferred content database
- Electronic software distribution
- Connections to third-party software applications and solutions
- Links to help-desk and training servers, along with a wide spectrum of tutorials
- Access via dedicated line or Internet
- WorldspanGo!® Mail and WorldspanGo!® Fax capabilities

The Worldspan organization was intended primarily to service large travel agencies.

Amadeus (Formerly System One)

Although Amadeus claimed to be the largest *global* travel distribution service, its U.S. market share had dropped to about 12 percent by 1998, making it the smallest major player among CRSs servicing American agents.[10] In contrast to Galileo International, which retained its traditional Apollo brand in most of the Americas, Amadeus folded the familiar System One nameplate into its worldwide brand.

System One began in 1981 as the CRS of Eastern Airlines, whereas Amadeus started out as a joint effort of Air France, Iberia, Lufthansa, and Scandinavian Airlines System (SAS); the latter group wanted to create an independent, European-based distribution and reservation system for the travel industry. In 1987, Amadeus and System One began to cooperate. The merger process was completed in February 1998, when Amadeus Global Travel Distribution (then owned by Air France, Iberia, Lufthansa, and Continental) became the sole owner of Miami, Florida-based Amadeus Global Travel Distribution LLC, the company that distributed and marketed System One Amadeus in North and Central America and the South Pacific. The nerve centers of Amadeus were in Madrid, Spain (marketing); Erding, Germany (operations); and Nice, France (customer support and development), with Miami serving as its North American headquarters.

In August 1998, Amadeus announced some details of Project Vista, its browser-based front office system. With Project Vista,

Amadeus boldly went where no CRS had gone before, giving agents the tools to incorporate the CRS information into an Internet environment. This meant that agents no longer had to make the awkward switch between making a reservation and accessing the Internet or e-mail any more—they could do it all through one conveniently integrated reservation screen. Project Vista was be tested in the United States and Canada beginning in November 1998.

Whether Amadeus was accessed via the Internet or a dedicated line, its services were built around the Amadeus Central System. It provided real-time access to schedules, fares, and rates of airlines, hotels, car rental companies, tour operators, and other travel vendors.

- Amadeus Air gave access to the schedules of more than 700 airlines, with reservation capabilities for 400 and last-seat availability for more than 260.
- Amadeus Hotels worked with almost 300 hotel companies, offering reservations for a combined total of 49,901 properties worldwide.
- Amadeus Cars featured more than 50 car rental companies representing 19,000 locations worldwide.
- Amadeus Rail provided access to Amtrak and Britrail.
- Amadeus Tours had 23 tour providers in the United States.
- Amadeus Cruise used Cruise Match 2000 to allow users to make real-time bookings for Royal Caribbean and Celebrity cruises.
- Amadeus Destination incorporated destination information and the ability to sell local leisure services.
- Amadeus Traveler was a combination of the PNR and customer profiles, allowing easy transfer of information from one to the other.
- Amadeus Fares allowed agents to display, compare, and sell more than 40 million fares for air, rail, and ground transportation.
- Amadeus Documents produced the full range of travel documents in both paper and electronic formats.

Amadeus Services for Travel Agencies

The services of the Amadeus Central System were delivered to agents through the MAXSys agency productivity software (APS), which included a variety of handy macros to speed up transactions. An add-on to this software was the Service Bureau Fare

Choice®, offering alternative, lower fare, and flight recommendations when compared to an existing itinerary or given a price to beat.

ExpressRes™ was a Windows-based productivity tool that removed the burden of having to know thousands of cryptic commands to query the Amadeus system.

Amadeus Services for Home-Based Agents

The HomePro was a Windows-based remote access program that was to be replaced by a remote version of Project Vista.

Amadeus Services for Corporate Users

The Corporate Circle® and Premium Corporate Circle® products included training, seminars, network opportunities, and discounts on Amadeus products. They also came with Corporate TripSolution™, an Internet- or intranet-based booking product through which travelers could book air, car, and hotel reservations online, with completed PNRs queued to the travel agency for quality control and ticketing. Add-ons included services such as:

- Availability displays biased to reflect company-wide policies and individual traveler preferences
- Low-fare searching and access to preferred vendors
- Policy Designer, to develop and/or improve travel policies

Amadeus Services for Consumers

Online Basic Consumers could connect with the Amadeus system at http://www.us.amadeus.com, where they had to enter the name of an Amadeus travel agency. Amadeus Online Basic was an excellent, low-cost way for agencies to get onto the Web quickly and without hassle.

Online Premium This marketing program featured a private-label Internet booking product—essentially a privately branded, customized booking site. In contrast to the Online Basic service, Online Premium gave Amadeus agencies the freedom to create their own content, including logo, agency description, and more.

Amadeus Business Strategy

Amadeus moved aggressively into new areas by acquiring vacation.com, at the time the world's largest Internet-enabled network of independent leisure travel agencies, with more than 8,400 members responsible for travel sales of more than $20 billion annually. Amadeus also bought a minority stake in One Travel, a top U.S. online travel Web site. In cooperation with Lycos Terra, it launched Rumbo, an online travel agency aimed at Spanish- and Portuguese-speaking countries of Europe and South America.

◼ What the Future Holds

None of the CRS services were ready, as of 1998, to cut the dedicated telephone lines that tied them to their agencies, but the time will come when these lines have to be abandoned to make way for Internet access. Agencies that need a separate modem to connect to the Internet will find that a less-than-satisfactory solution. CRS companies will probably enable agent access via the Internet with intranet and/or extranet solutions. Nevertheless, travel agents could not just wait for the CRS services to provide optimal Internet solutions; they had to find the best deals in this new technology by themselves.

◼ Summary

Online technology brought new competitors into the retail travel marketplace. CRS services adapted by offering novel services to both consumers and travel agents, though CRS services regarded their relationship with travel agents as key to their success. All four major CRS services were moving toward Internet compatibility.

Travelocity and Expedia were two of these competitors. Travel agents needed to understand the nature of these companies and their approaches.

The two dominant CRS services in the United States were SABRE and Apollo; Amadeus and Worldspan were minor competitors. All travel agents had to be familiar with the product lines of the two major companies.

End Notes

[1] Jim Frederick, "Fare Values? Trying to Net the Best Online Travel Deals," *Money*, 4 April 1998.

[2] Frederick, "Fare Values?"

[3] Ellie Knight, personal conversation with author, 1998.

[4] See **http://www.sabre.com/products/index.html.**

[5] Quoted in an interview with Diane Mayoros, *Wall Street Corporate Reporter.* Retrieved July 31, 1998, from **http://www.prnewswire.com/cnoc/GLCanalyt.html.**

[6] Mayoros, interview.

[7] Service description from Galileo International's Web site. Retrieved July 31, 1998, from **http://www.galileo.com/agencies/.**

[8] Galileo International, press release, 29 September 1998.

[9] Galileo International, press release, 29 May 1998.

[10] Joan M. Feldman, "CRSs on the Move," *Air Transport World* 35 (no. 5, May 1998): 73.

CHAPTER 3

Getting onto the Internet

Chapter Outline

Objectives

After completing this chapter, you should be able to:

- Define the term *Internet service provider*
- Describe the functions of browsers
- Understand the operation of Web portals
- Identify uses for intranets and extranets

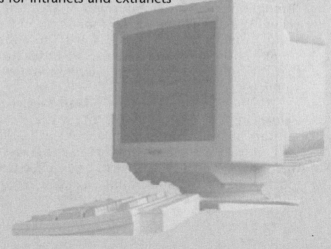

■ Introduction

Most personal computers in travel agencies use a modem that is hooked up to a dedicated telephone line, which provides a continuous connection to a CRS's mainframe computer. Although connected to an outside information provider, these computers or terminals are not connected to the Internet. To enable an Internet connection, most airline-installed computers require a separate modem.

Think of the Internet as a phone company switchboard. To make a phone call, you need a telephone connected by a wire to a phone company switchboard. To get online with a single computer, you need a modem-equipped computer or Internet-ready television connected to the server of an Internet service provider (ISP), portal, or gateway by telephone wires or cable television service wires. (Very few connections are actually direct to the Internet.) A stand-alone computer or group of computers can accomplish astonishing feats (database management, desktop publishing, spreadsheets, and word processing), but magic happens when the equipment is connected to the Internet with the help of a modem.[1] Although a majority of American households now have computers, not all of them have Internet connections. In terms of buying power, those who are online make cash registers ring in a big way. Needless to say, almost all businesses in the United States use computers, and most of them are connected to the Internet.

Once your computer is connected to an ISP's server, the browser software installed on your computer lets you use the Internet. The browser is your entry point into the Internet: It lets you see and use information stored in millions of computers throughout the world. Information accessed on the Internet is generally more abundant and more current than what a travel agent formerly had available. But be forewarned! The Internet supplies overwhelming amounts of indiscriminate information that the user has to sort out, interpret, and evaluate for accuracy and veracity.

The browser also lets you send and receive messages, chat, participate in discussion groups, and more. Add-on hardware and software allow you to make telephone calls, send faxes, and conduct videoconferences. Internet messaging (e-mail) is cheaper than faxing, and a Web site can be an effective tool for staying in touch with clients and promoting your services to a worldwide audience.

■ Internet Service Providers

Typically, an Internet service provider (ISP) delivers access to this magic kingdom, and a browser makes it come alive on your computer screen. The computer's modem uses a local telephone number established by the ISP (or by a company designated to provide such numbers for the ISP) to establish a connection to the ISP's computer—the *server*. Well-known ISPs in the United States are giant America Online, Earthlink, and MSN (the Microsoft Network); however, there are thousands of smaller ISPs, both national and local, to choose from. Cable modems connect a computer to the Internet via television cable (CATV). It is important to know that the Internet is accessible in a meaningful way only with a modem and the service of an ISP.

■ The World Wide Web

The World Wide Web (WWW, or W3, or the Web) is just one aspect of the Internet, but because of its capabilities, it has become the Net's major component, replacing many older text-only interfaces. Once you're online, you'll likely be cruising the Web. It appears on your screen complete with graphics, text, interactivity, audio, and video, depending on your computer's capabilities and your preferences.

■ Browsers

A computer must not only be connected to an ISP, but must also be equipped with a browser to process the information received from and sent to the Internet. The beauty of browsers is that they can access information originating from just about any online computer, regardless of its location and regardless of the format in which the information is stored. The most popular browsers in the United States for business are Netscape Communicator and Microsoft Internet Explorer: Both products are excellent and they are in many respects quite similar. Chances are that your computer has one or the other product built in, and most people stick to what their machines come with. However, a few variations may make a difference to sophisticated users.

For example, Microsoft's Internet Explorer provides videoconferencing, within its NetMeeting module; Netscape's Communicator 4.02 and higher Pro editions manage group scheduling, which may be important for people participating in countrywide or worldwide project groups. The biggest difference between the two products may be how the public perceives them, and particularly how it perceives the companies that produce them.

Web Portals

Many companies have attempted to provide a more versatile Internet starting point, complete with the latest news, weather, browsing, and searching. CATV companies, ISPs, and search-engine operators wanted to retain user interest beyond simple searches, and for this reason they created complete personalized services that supply e-mail, personalized news, access to chat and newsgroups, and often a personalized home page. This combination of services makes accessing and selecting information easier. This hot idea of 1998 was called a *Web portal,* which was supposed to be your rent-free home on the Internet. It appeared as soon as you logged on, and it stayed with you—in the background—throughout the day to make checking your mail, conducting searches, getting the latest news, taking the pulse of the stock market, and so on a matter of just a few keystrokes. Web portals gave lots of service, and in exchange, exposed users to their advertisers' and sponsors' messages.

The Web portal concept was created by AOL, the leading Internet service provider for consumers, and the format was adopted by many others, including search-engine sites. A CRS service might offer a Web portal especially to its travel agents. Although you may not want to use such a service, you ought to be familiar with the concept, as each of them prominently features travel services.

A Level Playing Field

The browser gives you the power to contact almost anybody in the world who has access to an online computer, and lets you receive messages from anybody in the world with online computer access. This universal access is one of the outstanding characteristics of the Internet, making it a reasonably level playing field for all users. Online computing encourages the collection and distribution of information. Because travel agencies are both seekers and providers of information, the more level playing field allows even small players to participate on somewhat equal terms with the "heavies." Diligent research skills and good Web site deployment empower agents to communicate inexpensively with a rapidly growing segment of the general public.

■ Intranets and Extranets

An *intranet* connects a company's computers to each other internally, making information stored on each one available to authorized users (see Figure 3-1). Employees can share software, and they can send and receive text, graphics, video, and sound within the intranet. Areas of an intranet that can be accessed by outsiders, such as vendors and clients, are called *extranets*. With the proper authorization, intranets can be accessed from desktops and laptops in the workplace, at home, and on the road. Intranets have become a very popular Internet application. According to a manager of Netscape Communications Corporation's enterprise markets, in 1997 "no one had heard of the intranet. Now, it has totally taken off." Netscape, the fast-growing developer of Internet browser technology, estimated that 80 percent of its business came from sales to intranets.[2] It is likely that much of the communication between travel agents and their computer reservation services will move from the CRSs' private networks to intranet or extranet technology.

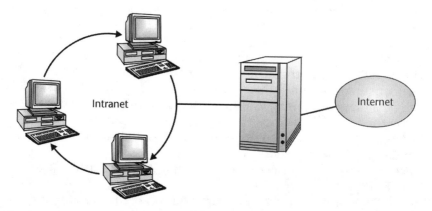

FIGURE 3-1 Intranet: The Web within

Intranets

For some corporations, an intranet offered a last frontier of cost reductions in the travel budget—reductions that went beyond obtaining the discounts that had already reduced travel expenses. A good corporate travel application would enforce company travel rules, regulations, and restrictions, and its automation would allow staff reductions at the corporate travel department as well as at the corporate travel agency. According to Hal Rosenbluth, chief executive officer of Rosenbluth International Travel headquartered in Philadelphia, Pennsylvania, intranets promised cost reductions of up to 30 percent. These applications allowed individual business travelers to connect to up-to-date travel information sources using their own desktop or laptop computers. Orders could be electronically transmitted via the Internet to the authorized travel agency, and from there (via the CRS or the Internet) to airlines, hotels, car rental agencies, and the like. The software that enabled this process also automated the issuance of travel documents, billing, and the production of reports for the agency and the corporation. This system reduced the need for human involvement in the transaction, other than that of the traveler.[3]

A good example of a company benefiting from travel services provided over an intranet was Charles Schwab & Co., a leading discount stock broker. According to a director of corporate travel at the San Francisco-based financial services company, "Schwab's travel division ... reduced its internal staff from 17 to 11 employees. It reduced telephone inquiries from 350 five-minute calls per day to 224 calls, each averaging three minutes or less. And the $1.6 million that Schwab saved from these measures last year went straight to the company's bottom line."[4] At Schwab's, an administrative assistant who booked travel for her boss, no longer had to call the travel office every time she had to make a choice or change. "[The intranet cut] down on the back-and-forth nature of the process, which ultimately can be aggravating, especially when you're not making the arrangements for yourself," she said.[5] Unlike consumer-oriented Internet booking engines, such as Expedia or Travelocity, corporate online systems permit companies to enforce their travel policies, including using preferred airlines or hotels with which the company has negotiated rates. Online corporate offerings included American Express Company's Interactive (AXI), Internet Travel Network's Global Manager, and a package from SABRE.

Schwab automated its entire travel management process using SABRE's Business Travel Solutions suite. Employees made reservations and ordered tickets online. They charged expenses using credit cards; the credit-card companies sent receipts via e-mail so that employees could download expense information automatically into an electronic expense form. Employees typed in only items for which they paid cash. Managers approved expense reports electronically, and the company electronically reimbursed both the credit-card company and the employees. Summary reports helped managers analyze both department and company-wide travel activity.

A corporate travel auditor hired by Schwab determined that companies in the San Francisco area pay, on average, 32 cents to 34 cents per mile for travel. Before implementing a full electronic management strategy, Schwab paid almost 40 cents per mile, Grant said. The company now pays 20 cents to 21 cents per mile.[6]

Intranet technology may help airlines and the Federal Aviation Authority (FAA) to streamline reporting and rule enforcement. Imagine the efficiencies and cost reductions for airlines and the government that would result from giving up paper forms and upgrading to Internet/intranet technology. For these same reasons, the Internal Revenue Service (IRS) opened its extranet doors to allow taxpayers to download IRS forms and publications, and to file returns electronically.

As we have seen, the corporate intranet's great advantages are increased efficiency and cost reduction. Because an intranet is a vehicle that selectively facilitates and streamlines communications among organizations and individuals, the traditional intermediary's role may become increasingly difficult. Steve Lohr wrote that "playing the middleman role on the Internet is going to be a tricky way to make a living. The essence of the Internet, after all, is that it enables people and business to connect directly—sidestepping intermediaries like distributors and retailers."[7]

Travel agencies heavily dependent on traditional airline ticket sales may draw a cautionary lesson from the price war that broke out among stock brokers on the Internet. In 1996, a *Los Angeles Times* article said that

> it sounds as if legions of America's hyper-caffeinated baby boomers are about to hang up on their fathers' cronies at the Merrill Lynch trust department and begin trading stocks at their PCs. Unlike the way it is with a lot of conventional wisdom on our wired future, this actually could happen. The increase in competition has already punctured the high price of trades so dramatically that the transaction cost need no longer be a consideration. At a full-service broker, the purchase of 500 shares of computer networking

giant Cisco Systems could cost more than $300 (commission), a big deal. At the least expensive Internet brokerage today, the cost is a flat $12.[8]

Extranets

When a company's intranet, typically containing information in database form, is opened to suppliers, clients, and other selected outside parties via the Internet, these outside links form an *extranet*. Detroit's automakers tested the Automotive Network Exchange (ANX), an extranet that securely interconnected automotive industry trading partners. The goals of ANX were to increase productivity and quality control, and to reduce cost by faster and more direct communications. Similar applications are likely to surface in the travel and tourism industry, particularly in the fields of large-scale meeting and convention management and tour operation. A vice president of product marketing at SABRE Travel Information Network stated that "the threat of technology supplanting the relationships between travel agents and their loyal customers is a concern only if agents refuse to change with the technology. To borrow a phrase from Winston Churchill, 'the only thing to fear is fear itself.' Never fear because *you* are the experts in travel, and you can leverage technology to your advantage."

Corporations also use extranet technology to give employees access to specialized databases that are not available to casual Internet users. Such services often provide highly specialized, continually updated information from proprietary databases of business topics. The SABRE Group's SABRExplorer was a proprietary database in this vein. Its purpose was fast delivery of real-time travel information. It consisted of data collected by the SABRE Group and it was available only to SABRE agents who participated in the company's extranet.

The Internet and its intranet and extranet extensions, together with the World Wide Web, were the technologies that caused the traditional travel buyer-seller model to evolve in ways not previously imagined. Forward-thinking agents used these tools to offer value-added services that would grow both their own and their clients' businesses. Imaginatively used, the Internet enabled travel agencies to negotiate better rates, to access valuable information more quickly, to find travel options that met specific client needs better, and to put their focus where it should be: on the customer.

■ Summary

An Internet service provider is usually needed to gain access to the Internet. The World Wide Web is the most popular area of the Internet. Browsers are programs that handle information coming from and going to the Internet, including the World Wide Web. Web portals give complete Internet services as soon as you are connected. Intranets and extranets underlie many corporate travel programs offered by CRS services.

End Notes

[1] An excellent discussion of basic Internet architecture can be found at http://navigators.com/internet_architecture.html.

[2] *Orange County Register,* 21 May 1997.

[3] Corporate intranets capable of handling travel services attracted the attention of some big players: American Express and Microsoft planned to introduce intranet software that would allow users easy access to American Express travel services while giving management the ability to capture all data necessary to control expenses. This intranet service was to be called SABRE Business Travel Solutions (BTI).

[4] Carol Sliwa, "Schwab Saves with 'Net Travel Planning," *Computerworld* 32 (no. 15, April 13, 1998): 41.

[5] Sliwa, 41.

[6] Sliwa, 41.

[7] Steve Lohr, "Profiting as a Business-to-Business Middleman on the Internet Is Tricky," *New York Times,* 19 May 1997.

[8] Jon D. Markman, "Newest Trick of the Trade," *Los Angeles Times,* 29 October 1996, D1.

CHAPTER 4

Time Management for the Online Agent

Chapter Outline

Objectives

After completing this chapter, you should be able to:

- Discuss the need for added value other than convenience
- Understand that the new environment requires a new work model
- Set schedules, goals, and priorities
- Recognize the need for continuing education

■ Introduction

In previous chapters it has been suggested that CRS-based distribution of services via travel agencies may lose dominance as the prime conduit of travel services between vendors and customers. Agents have become just one of many distribution systems for travel services. There were two major reasons for this development:

1. Internet technology offered vendors attractive new distribution channels. Airlines, gravely aware of the almost 20 percent of gross income they had been spending on distribution, began to reduce this expense by dealing directly with frequent flyers and Fortune 500 corporations, by further cutting or eliminating travel agent commissions, and by promoting ticketless travel. Big hotel chains, car rental companies, and tour operators gladly switched from using expensive CRSs to using lower-cost Internet channels to distribute services. Convention and visitor bureaus, tourist offices, and smaller vendors also embraced the Internet because it offered them, for the first time, a cost-effective alternative to distribution via expensive mail, fax, and phone channels.

2. Internet technology offered travelers direct access to vast information databases, some of which were once the exclusive domain of travel agents (see Figure 4-1). Not only are vast sites such as Microsoft Expedia and Travelocity full of information and ever-smarter booking engines, but they are also open around the clock. Suddenly, even convenience is not a travel agency exclusive any more.

These trends made it vital for travel agents to add value to the services they sold other than geographic convenience. To compete successfully in the online environment, they also needed to step up their sales activities. The imperatives of innovation and increased sales and marketing at the agency and agent levels shaped the schedules, goals, and priorities of most agents. Formerly, 75 percent of an agent's time might have been spent on the phone with clients and vendors, processing reservations; much of this work has become automated, with clients either using their online services or using the phone to connect with voice-recognition reservation centers. Inevitably, agents will have time on their hands either to develop new, high-yield business, or to improve their solitaire-playing skills. Switching from "travel reservation taker" to "travel marketing and sales specialist" requires behavioral changes.

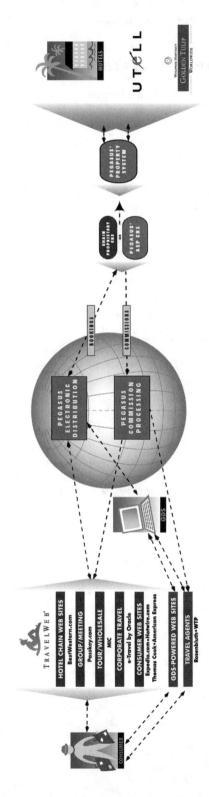

FIGURE 4-1 One of the many ways in which consumers can access travel information. (Courtesy Pegasus Systems Inc., Dallas, TX)

■ The Entrepreneurial Online Agent

Before you consider such a change, you need to find out what you're best at, and how you can apply your set of skills in this new environment. Take a good look at yourself and find out whether you want to face the challenge of fundamental change. If you're perfectly happy handling reservations whenever the phone happens to ring, you may want to stop reading this text right now—but start worrying about job security in a line of work that is increasingly automated.

If you think you can learn new skills, though, go out and convince clients that you and your company can create and arrange travel services better than they can. If you think you can create new services, read on.

■ The New Agent's Basic Tool Kit

The successful agent will work in an active, entrepreneurial, and creative arena, rather than in a reactive (waiting for the phone to ring) employee mode. Entrepreneurial agents will emphasize working smarter, rather than working harder. Using software to your advantage is an important part of smart work, and your schedule must consistently allow time for continuous learning. Technology changes quickly and the simple truth that "he who rests, rusts" has never been more true than today. The basic skills for the entrepreneurial online travel agent include the ability to handle:

- Computer reservation systems
- Travel products and destinations
- Marketing and sales
- Word processing
- Spreadsheets
- Database management
- Desktop publishing
- Presentation tools
- Time management
- E-mail
- Web searching
- Web site authoring and/or editing

Agents selling to corporate customers also need to be familiar with their CRS's capability to provide services via an intranet.

You will use these skills in a multitasking environment. Only the last five skills in the preceding list, and their specific applications for the retail travel industry, are covered in this text. Inexpensive classes covering computer literacy are available at many community colleges, both as traditional classes and as online courses.

It is important to recognize that the planning process goes hand in hand with skills development. Obviously, you cannot schedule sales calls to corporations before you know how to pitch intranet travel solutions. Rather than creating a grandiose plan, begin by budgeting time on a daily plan, with the goal of getting you more in front of sympathetic customers likely to buy high-yield products.

■ Planning, Goal Setting, and Prioritizing

Once you are used to creating and following a daily plan, you may want to advance to a weekly schedule, and later to a monthly or even semi-annual procedure. However, it is strongly recommended that you start simply, with daily plans and goals—you have to learn to walk before you can run.

At the Close of the Day

Take 10 or 15 minutes to plan and organize the next day. Establish a schedule and set some goals, such as contacting at least 10 important clients and finding a class to acquire a missing skill. This way, tomorrow you can hit the ground running, rather than scratching your head in the morning wondering what the day will bring. Prioritize daily goals by creating an "A" list of people you must contact no matter what, a "B" list of people you ought to be in touch with, and a "C" list of people who should hear from you. A good schedule that allocates two hours for a Chamber of Commerce mixer tells you right away that you're not going to have a chance to contact C-list people individually—but maybe you can reach them with a broadcast message.

Your "A" folder may include several categories of "must be in touch with today" companies and people. For instance: (1) calls to clients about urgently pending matters (including crises and emergencies); (2) calls to clients with good prospects for higher-yield orders; and (3) calls to vendors and information providers with whom you may be developing new products.

Your "B" folder may list the people to whom you'd like to talk because you think they have potential business. It could also contain an item: "need to look up online courses about presentation tools."

On your "C" list are contacts who need attention, but not necessarily today. Your C folder may also contain ideas that help you cobble together brief but frequent newsletters or sales announcements.

When this text uses the term *calls,* it doesn't necessarily mean telephone calls. A call can be a personal visit, a phone call, an e-mail message, a fax, or a memo via snail mail. The contact medium depends on customer preference, time available, and the type of message and information you are dealing with.

Although it is important to realize than not everything can be accomplished as planned, this realization is no excuse for forgoing planning. You must produce a prioritized outline of tomorrow's activities and goals and a schedule, and stick to them.

The Early Bird Gets the Worm

Your workday starts at home, where you listen to your phone messages and fire up your PC to review critical passenger name records (PNRs), read your e-mail, absorb general and travel-related news, and create messages for your clients. This is your first chance of the day to let online technology and multitasking empower you to work smarter. Use your hi-tech tools to access, absorb, sort, prioritize, and prepare information to quicken your clients' decision cycles. Put another way, use online technology to shorten time to market. For many people, this early-morning approach is very productive, because their energy level is high; their focus is sharp; their minds are as yet uncluttered by all the matters that will occur throughout the day; and their time is uninterrupted, due to the merciful absence of phone calls and office chit-chat. Use the early part of the day to fill your A, B, and C folders.

1. Sort incoming phone messages, e-mail, Web downloads, and news in appropriate folders. In the same folders, file the information (such as forthcoming birthdays and anniversaries) that you glean continually from your client database. At this time, don't make phone calls; stay focused on getting organized. Simply add all urgent information and messages to your A folder. Inability to complete this step without making phone

calls or responding to e-mail messages may suggest that you are subconsciously unwilling to get organized.

2. Connect collected information with the clients on your A, B, and C lists, and reorganize folder contents accordingly. Your database may tell you that a client on your B list will be celebrating his 40th birthday soon, so you should send a card today. Therefore, the action of getting and mailing a card advances to the A folder, to assure that this will be done today.

3. Compose your actual messages (phone calls, e-mail, faxes, and memos via regular mail).

4. From folder A, which includes crisis and emergency management, send out your first messages via e-mail and fax. Time permitting, service folders B and C similarly, otherwise, get to B and C later.

Scrap Time

Now that you have probably accomplished two hours' worth of work in less than one hour, relax, have breakfast, take a walk, or go to the gym. When you later commute to the agency, think of how you could make better use of "scrap" time. You probably waste bits of it every day when you are:

- Waiting (for a client, for a meeting, for the phone to ring, for a doctor's appointment)
- Driving (stuck in traffic, commuting)
- Doing non-thought-intensive activities (jogging, riding your exercycle, sorting brochures)

Rebecca L. Morgan suggests that you make use of this scrap time by:

- Planning your next sales call
- Reviewing what you think your client needs
- Critiquing your last sales call
- Visualizing your next sales call
- Listening to a motivational or informational presentation
- Writing a quick note to a client or someone you just met
- Catching up on reading
- Updating and refining your daily schedule and goals
- Mining your client database

Putting scrap time to good use takes some forethought and planning. Obviously, you'll have to have reading and listening materials available during scrap time if you are to make use of them. Likewise, you'll want to have client lists, your schedule, and goals with you to work on some of the other items. Last but not least, never be caught without a notebook and a pencil.[1]

Office Pressures

Upon arrival at the office, you will have to update your schedule, as well as your folders, as you receive more messages. Now that the business day has really started, answering the phone becomes a top priority—most clients hate to leave messages. Talk to your clients and handle their business. But the moment you're off the phone, go back to your A folder and take care of its contents, one by one, according to the way you prioritized them. Try to make phone calls early, and send e-mails and faxes out before you and your clients get too frazzled.

■ Time Is Money—Use It Efficiently

- Use e-mail to arrange personal and phone appointments. Your client will be ready and focused.
- Just say no when colleagues distract you with idle talk; say, "Sorry, I'm busy selling."
- Address groups of clients in the form of mailing lists, parties, seminars, or training sessions.

As the hours vanish one by one, you'll realize that you cannot reach all the goals you set unless you really kick up your speed a few notches. *Don't!* Your time is spent much more productively if you stay fully focused on your current task and trust your previous prioritizing, as opposed to worrying over what you need to get done by the end of the day. In fact, reserve your last half-hour for reviewing your day. Think about how long you were in front of clients, and how long in front of the water cooler or the solitaire screen. How can you get more client time? By delegating certain tasks to support staff? By becoming a more efficient computer user through training? By shifting from phone messages to e-mail? Having reviewed the day, you can adjust tomorrow's schedule and goals to a more manageable level, and you can begin to add long-term projects such as training and new product development.

■ Summary

Online technology changed the role of the agency in the distribution of travel services. To prosper, you must adapt. Take charge of your time by developing schedules and priorities. They help you to make a successful transition from traditional order taker to New-Economy entrepreneur.

End Notes

[1] Rebecca L. Morgan, "Salvaging Sales Scrap Time," *American Salesman* 41, no. 10 (October 1966): 8.

CHAPTER 5

Gathering Information

Chapter Outline

Objectives
After completing this chapter, you should be able to:
- Set up and use client databases
- Understand uniform resource locators (URL)
- Use search engines
- Use personalized news services
- Be familiar with listservs and mailing lists

■ Client Information

Hunting and gathering took up most of the time of early humans—and as we moved beyond the industrial age into the information age, it seemed that we had come full circle. Instead of grubbing for berries, nuts, and roots, though, we began gathering information on the Internet. The wealth of information available through the Internet is awe-inspiring, confusing, and overwhelming. Cyber-literate travel agents bring order and sense to this information chaos. They process information efficiently to market it to discrete groups of clients, and to prepare travel plans of unprecedented accuracy and breadth. Using the Internet, a travel agent can easily and quickly gather information about any itinerary, even one that includes obscure destinations and special events.

Many clients expect travel agents to do the grubbing for them. Yes, they could gather it on their own computers at home or at the office, but who has the time? And who knows how to do it efficiently or how to evaluate it professionally? Few but cyber-literate travel agents. They not only know their clients' needs and wants, but they also know how to retrieve relevant information from the Internet, how to process that information within the reservation system environment to provide the client with a total package, and how to sell via the Internet.

■ Client Database

The most important source of information belongs to you: it is your client database. Client information is best stored in a database that can be queried in a variety of ways. A good client database ought to be given daily massages during which you update client records and compare newly available information with the needs and wants of your clients. A Web site produces inquiries that must be added to the database. The goal of this ongoing work is one-on-one marketing and selling, a technique that is a natural offshoot of the Internet and of database technology. Many software companies offer prepackaged databases, some of which are designed especially for retail travel agencies.

Simplicity

The client database should be at the fingertips of all agents so that they can update, edit, and use it whenever they want. Each agent will need training before he or she can use a database easily, effectively, and efficiently.

Easy Access

In most multitasking environments, the database is never more than a few clicks away.

Versatility

The database must be amenable to frequent design changes so that it is adaptable to changing requirements. Users must be able to implement those changes quickly, without outside help and without risking data loss. Changes may include addition of new reports (mailing lists and content of mailings; lists of birthdays, anniversaries, etc.), design changes, and new entries. (Please note that learning database management is not within the purview of this book. Some of your continuing education effort is well spent in this area.)

Usage

A database earns its keep by continually supporting marketing and sales efforts. Easy access and simplicity lead to frequent use of the database, which should contain at least the fields shown in Figure 5-1 on page 56. In addition to the fields shown in Figure 5-1, you may want to include psychographic traits of your clients, Web sites you think the client would enjoy, and whatever else you think may be relevant and lead to sales.

Using the Database

Use your database to support your information-gathering efforts on the Internet, and for more conventional marketing and public relations efforts (such as the mailing of birthday cards, anniversary wishes, etc.). Working with the Internet will bring new clients to your agency, and the database will help you serve them (see Figure 5-2 on page 57).

The Database and the Web

The Internet and especially the World Wide Web tend to be personal, chatty environments. The casual style of this medium is ideally suited to travel sales and services. Internet-savvy agents use

Personal Information	Business Information
First Name	Company Name
Last Name	Department
Title	Title
Street	Street
City	City
Zip	Zip
State	State
Phone	Phone
Fax	Fax
E-Mail	E-Mail
Web Site	Web Site
Birthdate (MM/DD/YY)	
Birthday (MM/DD)	
Anniversary (MM/DD)	
Passport Expiration (MM/DD/YY)	
Past Vacation Destinations	Past Business Destinations
Hobbies, Special Interests	Clubs, Organizations
	Conventions, Trade Fairs

FIGURE 5-1 Sample fields in a client database

these characteristics to their advantage: They are in a continuous dialogue with their clients about relevant travel information as it becomes available. That's why it is so important to have information about each client's needs. Some agencies are using the resulting one-on-one marketing to replace printed and mailed newsletters with information streams that are personalized for each client.

Although a travel agency may not think it can afford the programs necessary to automate the process of sending personalized information to clients, a personalized but nonautomatic approach

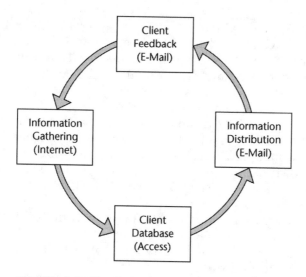

FIGURE 5-2 Circular relationship between database, information gathering, and information distribution

is possible. In fact, this approach may suit the personalities of travel agency clients better anyway. A section later in this chapter discusses how to use a client database to market information found on the Internet.

■ Information Central: The Internet

A most important part of your job is to provide good information. As the dissemination of good information about flights and reservations becomes automated, the Internet becomes your most important tool for gathering information about other aspects of travel. You get better and more up-to-date information from the Web than from most other sources, such as CRS services, books, and journals. Of course, nothing replaces personal experience, and the blending of destination knowledge with the latest tidbits available on the Net keeps your own body of knowledge fresh. Unfortunately, everybody else who uses the Internet can get as much information as you can; you will have to work smart to stay ahead of your clients!

The World Wide Web

Accessing information on the user-friendly World Wide Web is easy but time-consuming. You need to learn to find information efficiently and to evaluate its accuracy and usefulness. Instead of knowing city codes and fares by heart, you'll become expert in finding and using the best Web addresses (URLs) and search engines. City codes are static (FAT will always be Fresno) and the Web is dynamic, so your new expertise will be challenged again and again by this rapidly changing and growing medium. As long ago as 1996, *Internet World* estimated that the number of Web pages doubles every 12 to 15 months. Part of your challenge is to keep abreast of what's new and important. You will inevitably end up with your own list of reliable, useful sites and URLs, but Appendix A contains a selected list of Web sites worth visiting to get you started.

The other part of your challenge is to think critically when searching the Web (see Figure 5-3). Don't just trust anything you find—consider a site's authority and objectivity before using information you find there.

Uniform Resource Locators

Information is located in files stored electronically on the computers connected by the Internet. The names or "addresses" of these files are called *uniform resource locators* (URLs). Each article, database, newsgroup, file, or other Internet piece of information has its own URL consisting of clearly distinguishable sections.

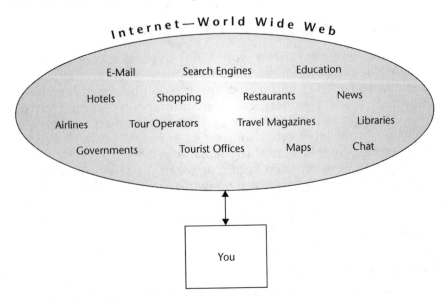

FIGURE 5-3 Your place in cyberspace: Unlimited choices

URLs are case-sensitive; that is, they must be entered as shown. Most URLs use lower case only.

(1)**http://**(2)**www.**(3)**iflyswa.**(4)**com/**(5)**herb/**(6)**herbie.**(7)**html**

(1) **http://** These letters describe the service you are reaching. Typically they are "http," which stands for HyperText Transfer Protocol.

(2) **www.** These letters indicate a service on the Internet; in this example, the World Wide Web.

(3) **iflyswa.** This is the address of the host computer. Southwest Airlines chose "I fly SWA" as its easy-to-remember host name.

(4) **com/** These suffix letters are part of the host's address (see the list of suffixes in Appendix C). One convention regarding these suffixes or extensions is used in the United States, and another in all other countries. Recognizing some of these extensions may help you avoid wild goose chases when searching for information.

(5) **herb/** Name of a directory

(6) **herbie.** Name of a file within the directory

(7) **html** Name of the computer language in which the file is written; in this example, HyperText Markup Language (htm or html).

You can access a file by jumping to it with the aid of a hyper-link, by typing its URL into the appropriate window of your browser or portal, or by finding it with the help of a search engine. Regardless of how you access a file, you can always store its name in your bookmarks to reach it faster the next time.

Bookmarks

Microsoft's Internet Explorer calls its bookmarks "Favorites," and all you need to do to add a Web site or page to your list of frequently visited and/or important Web addresses is to click on "Favorites" and then on "Add." This procedure adds the particular URL to your list. The procedure for Netscape is essentially the same, except that bookmarks are called "Bookmarks."

Web Information Management

If your list of bookmarked URLs becomes extensive, you may want to keep track of interesting sites with a database containing the type of information shown in Appendix A. It may be easier to match Web sites with client needs with the assistance of such a searchable database. You can also cross-reference your client database with this new keyword database.

Hyperlinks

Hyperlinks are an integral part of the World Wide Web, and you will see them used liberally throughout most Web pages. Hyperlinks can be in the form of text or graphics. Either way, your cursor will change from an arrow to a pointing hand when it is over a hyperlink. As soon as you click on a hyperlink, the linked file will appear on your screen. Often, you are linked to a file in a subdirectory of a site, and you can navigate your way to the site's main or home page by clicking on the word "home."

There are millions of URLs, with thousands more added weekly. We call a person's or organization's page (or series of pages) a *Web site,* and the first page the *home* or *index* page. Each page or file has its own URL. In other words, you can select the home page of an organization, and from there find directions to the page containing the information you are seeking. You can also go directly to the URL of a specific page of an organization's Web site.

Selecting a Site by Typing Its URL

Both Microsoft Internet Explorer and Netscape Communicator feature auto fill-in of URLs; that is, you only need to fill in the host computer's name. For example, you want to find passport information, so you check the Web site of the U.S. State Department. Its URL is state.gov, which is all you have to type if you are using one of the major browsers. However, users of older browsers may have to type the entire URL: **http://www.state.gov/**. As soon as you hit "Enter" after typing the URL, the browser goes into action and (using the protocol contained in the URL) connects you with the Web page uniquely identified by this URL (see Figure 5-4).

In our State Department example, the home page of this huge organization's Web site leads to its various departments and services. As you move your mouse over the various graphic and text areas, you will notice that the pointing arrow sometimes turns into a hand. Whenever the hand appears, you are pointing to an active link to another page. Use your mouse to point to the "scrabble board" picture (it contains the word *passport*), and then click.

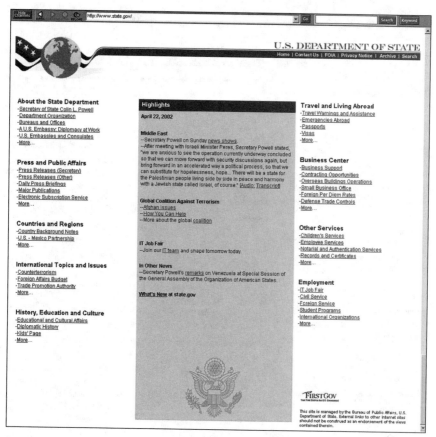

FIGURE 5-4 U.S. State Department main Web page,
http://www.state.gov/ (Courtesy U.S. Department of State)

Depending on the speed of your modem and the general status of
the Internet at the time of your click, your screen will sooner or
later fill with the State Department's "services" page. You note that
the URL in your browser's location window has changed from
http://www.state.gov/ (as in Figure 5-4) to http://www.state.gov/
travel/ (see Figure 5-5 on page 62).

This page serves as an index to the many services of the department. As you move your mouse, you will see that your arrow again
changes into a hand as you move over the many items listed. Notice that the URLs to which each one of these links would lead you
are shown in the bar just below your browser's image. Move your
pointer over the word "passports," and the URL of http://travel.
state.gov/passport_services.html appears below the active screen
of your browser (see Figure 5-6 on page 63). Click on the word

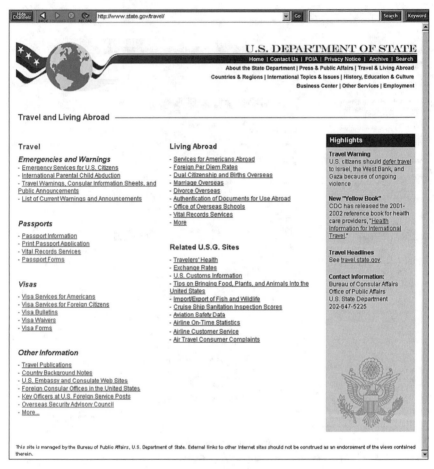

FIGURE 5-5 Screen from U.S. Department of State travel services Web area, http://www.state.gov/travel/ (Courtesy U.S. Department of State)

"passports" and soon the new page will appear on your screen. This page again gives you a choice of directions to go, from "Passports the Easy Way" to "Frequently Asked Questions."

Obviously, it would be much faster to go to the page http://travel.state.gov/passport_services.html directly, rather than wading through the various layers of the State Department's Web site. Therefore, you will want to add important URLs to your list of bookmarks. The next time you need to find passport information, you simply go to Favorites/Bookmarks and click on the State Department's Passport Information listing. Voilà, this Web page appears on your screen.

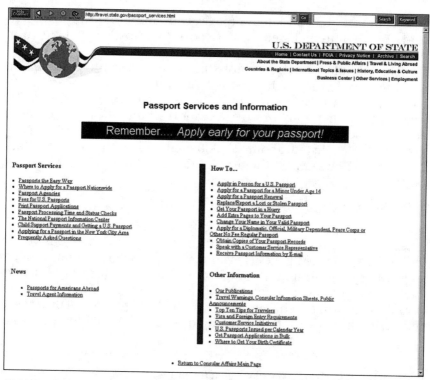

FIGURE 5-6 Screen from U.S. Department of State passport services Web area, http://travel.state.gov/passport_services.html (Courtesy U.S. Department of State)

■ Search Engines

When you don't know the URL of the page containing the information you're seeking, you turn to a *search engine,* the "phone directories" of the Internet. Almost all browsers offer easy access to search services. Using the previous example, you would click on "Search" and enter the word "passport" in the window following the words "net search with (name of search engine)." You may have a choice of search engines, and these choices are discussed later in this section. At this point, don't worry about which search engine you're using—just enter "passport" and click on "Search." Depending on which search engine your browser chooses to do the search, you end up with different displays and listings, but you may not see any of the State Department URLs discussed in the preceding section. This is because the engine is simply listing all sites where it found the word *passport*. The search engine HotBot found almost 90,000 matches (pages containing the word *passport*) and the first item listed is "Passport to Knowledge: Live from Mars!"

This simple exercise demonstrates the need for precision in searches: To do an efficient, effective, and productive search, you must narrow the scope of your queries as much as possible. Try "passport application" or "U.S. passport information," and you'll begin to see the State Department pages located earlier. (The HotBot search listed about 17,000 matches with the U.S. State Department, but ranked them in 23rd place.)

Finding Information with Search Engines

Search engines are the tools to find what you are looking for. Effective searching is an important time saver, but an extensive list of frequently visited pages is even better, as it avoids some searches altogether. Keep in mind, though, that any static directory (such as bookmarks) becomes obsolete quickly because the Internet is such a rapidly growing medium, as illustrated in Figure 5-7. This caveat applies with full force to the listing of URLs in Appendix A as well.

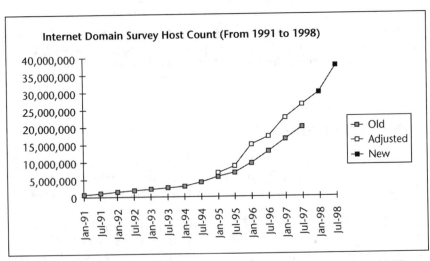

FIGURE 5-7 Growth of domains (URLs) worldwide from 1991 to 1998

Another way to reduce search time is simply to type the name of the company into the browser. Thus, you can reach the adventure travel company *OARS* by entering "oars," or, if you use an older browser, by entering its complete URL: **http//www.oars.com/**.

If this does not yield results, try "OARS"; if this also fails, let the search engine look for "oars."

Although most air, cruise, and rail lines; tour operators; tourist offices; hotel chains; and the like have Web sites (for examples, see Appendix A), you may not have their URLs handy. However, Web information is generally more up-to-date and therefore more accurate than printed brochures, and a look at a company's Web site ought to be your first step before requesting or giving information about a particular travel service. The Internet's information-gathering capabilities make it an indispensable tool for travel professionals. Many Web sites are more versatile, as well as more up-to-date, than printed materials. Some companies also offer regular updates on new developments.

Before investigating the nitty-gritty of searching, you need to know how search engines work. Each search engine sends out electronic "spiders" and "crawlers" that continually look into every nook and cranny of the expanding Internet. Depending on their instructions, they may harvest everything they find (complete content of all Web and other Internet sites), or may pick only the tastier stuff. Limited pickings may include a portion of the content, or only the titles and descriptions of Web pages, or only information that has been added and updated since the last crawl-by. Each bit of information sent home by these busy crawler programs is automatically indexed and stored.

Each search engine has its own way of indexing this vast influx of information: some indexes favor recently added or updated pages; others favor pages where the indexed word or words occur often. This indexing allows the search engine to display the results of your search according to a relevance ranking. When you search, the engine will compare your request with its index, not with what is actually available on the Internet at the time of your search. Therefore, your search results will vary from search engine to search engine and from day to day.

Regardless of which engine you use, specific and detailed queries produce the best results. Ask for "Paris Hotels Left Bank" (161 matches in HotBot), not for "Paris hotels" (11,392 matches in HotBot). Learn and use the special commands and techniques each search engine offers, such as Boolean logic (most search engines have help pages that explain their particular wording and character-use requirements). Although each search engine uses a different query format to apply this logic, the basic idea is to link your words with AND, OR, and NOT. It may be better to look for "desert AND resorts" than for "desert resorts," and for "desert AND resorts AND Arizona" than for "desert resorts in Arizona."

The following subsections describe a few of the most popular search engines by type: search engines, subject directories, and meta search engines. A continuously updated list of major search engines and their characteristics can be found at **http://infopeople. berkeley.edu/search/tools.html**.

AltaVista (http://altavista.com)

AltaVista boasts that its search engine collects the complete content of all sites. Consequently, if AltaVista can't find it, it probably is not on the Web. Multiple-word searches are much improved if the string of words is enclosed in quotes. Looking up the term *New York City* returns more than 76 million items, an impossible number to comb through. The term "New York City" returns more than 300,000 items—an improvement, but still too many items to review. Clicking on "Refine Search" allows additional narrowing of the search results. Using AltaVista's zones may produce better results than a general search.

Google (http://www.google.com)

Google offers the largest index of Web sites, and it presents its findings with the most popular sites at the top of the list. This ranking feature, which is a unique characteristic of Google, is based on the number of links a page has (that is, a link from page A to page B counts as a point for B and thus increases the ranking of page B). Moreover, an important, high-quality site will receive a higher rank, which Google remembers each time it conducts a search. This technique usually yields useful results very quickly.

HotBot (http://hotbot.lycos.com)

HotBot's advantage is its fast spiders that cruise around the Internet every two weeks. This may be important when you need to look at the latest additions to or updates of Web sites. Another time-sensitive HotBot feature is the choice to limit the search to sites that are not older than a given time that you select. This option is very useful when looking for travel information; after all, who wants to know about events in Boston three months ago?

Subject Directories

Although subject directories allow searching of the entire Internet, their strength is breaking down your search by category.

Yahoo (http://yahoo.com/) offers specialized areas within which to conduct searches. In addition, this engine allows you to search within geographic areas (World Yahoo!s and Yahoo! Metros).

Specialized Search Engines

The Scour (http://scour.com) search engine, designed by UCLA students, looks only for multimedia files: images, audio, and video. It is an excellent example of a specialized search engine.

Shopping Robots

A variety of search engines specifically geared to find products for sale on the Web have appeared. They make comparison shopping for common products and services a breeze. Junglee (http://shoptheWeb.amazon.com/stw.template/home.html) is obviously within the amazon.com fold. MySimon (http://www.mysimon.com), Bottom Dollar Shopping Agent (http://www.bottomdollar.com), and Shopfind (http://www.shopfind.com) are also leading shopping robots. Although travel is not yet a listed category on some of these sites, Bidders' Edge (http://www.biddersedge.com) has a travel category.

▪ Meta Search Engines

A meta search engine looks for matches in several search engines at once. Dogpile (http://www.dogpile.com) and MetaCrawler (http://www.metacrawler.com/index_metafind.html) both search multiple search engines simultaneously.

▪ The Invisible Net

An estimated two-thirds of content available on the Internet is hidden from easy view because it is stored in databases that cannot be located with a simple search. For example, suppose that you're trying to find out whether a small hotel in Switzerland, where a client wants to stay, accepts credit cards. A simple Google search does not provide this information. However, by going to the Swiss Hotel Association's database (a list of member hotels), you can access complete information about credit card acceptance at any member hotel in Switzerland.

Limited-Access Search Engines

As part of the SABRE CRS, SABRE AgentExplorer^{SM} is a private (password-secured) service that allows agents quick and easy access to Internet travel content. In contrast to the publicly available search engines mentioned earlier, the content of SABRE Agent-Explorer^{SM} has been prequalified to ensure that it is kept up-to-date, so that it will remain a productive tool for travel agents.

The content of AgentExplorer is grouped into ten main categories:

1. Destination Information
2. Maps
3. Weather
4. Hotels & Lodging
5. Rental Cars & Ground Transportation
6. Rail
7. Cruises
8. Publications
9. Shipment Tracking
10. Discounts and Deals

Personalized News Services

These programs provide you with a steady stream of mentions of your topic(s) in articles, Web pages, and so on. In other words, a personalized news service automates your searches. As the president of AltaVista Internet Software, Inc., pointed out, "As the Web continues to grow, a simple search query returns tens of thousands of results. The *AltaVista* search index is comprehensive, but users can feel overwhelmed by so many results." An AltaVista news release further explained the need for personalized news services: "[W]ith the addition of *LiveTopics* to the *AltaVista* search service, we are solving this problem. *LiveTopics* is a simple, intuitive tool for managing users' searches, and a faster, more effective way to pinpoint the information they need as well as learn about a new field of knowledge."[1]

Personalized services such as the "LiveTopics" feature of AltaVista Search simplify advanced searches of the Web by organizing thousands of results into useful topic categories and bringing structure and meaning to the results. For example, a search for the term "ATM" brings up references to 400,000 Web pages using that acronym. LiveTopics results appear in clear, concise topic categories. You can quickly zero in on Web pages discussing *asynchronous transfer mode networking* or *automated teller machines.*

AltaVista Search was one of the most popular search technologies on the Web, providing comprehensive and high-performance Internet search service to end users. Since 1995, both search services and sites and uses thereof proliferated rapidly; AltaVista got more than 5 billion hits in its first year of service. The frantic search for loyal customers by Internet service providers (ISPs) and search engines spawned another type of business that bundled services such as personalized news and search capabilities. This is the Web portal discussed in chapter 3.

▨ Mailing Lists

A *mailing list* is a computer program that automatically distributes messages among a list of subscribers. A mailing list has an e-mail (listserv) address, and mail sent to this address is distributed automatically to all subscribers. Participation in some lists is screened; in others, participation is automatic upon sign-up. Once you subscribe to a mailing list, you will receive copies of all the messages that people on the list find of interest (see Figure 5-8 on page 70 for a sample from Google Groups).

Many newsgroups and listservs started out on the Usenet, which predated the Web. Usenet was text-only, and a special search engine, "dejanews.com," was used to find appropriate groups of messages. In early 2001, Google, Inc., a leading search engine and index, acquired Dejanews.com. When the full Deja Usenet archive is added to Google's inventory, more than 500 million archived messages will become accessible and searchable.

To find discussion groups, visit Google's group site at **http:// groups.google.com**. There you can search for newsgroups by topic. This site allows you to search, read, and participate in a myriad of discussion forums, in English and in many other languages. This multilinguistic aspect may be of special interest to agents serving non-English-speaking clients.

Another excellent service to access discussion groups and newsgroups is Talkway (**http://talkway.com**). It works like a directory-based search engine and offers a special access channel for Java-enabled machines.

FIGURE 5-8 Sample travel discussion group from **http://groups.google. com/groups?hl=en&lr=&safe=off&group=rec.travel. bed%2Bbreakfast** (Courtesy Google, Inc.)

■ World Wide Wait

These visits to the Internet and the World Wide Web have shown the incredible array of information available on the Net, but they may also have exposed you to some of the Internet's problems: namely, information overload and slow data transmission.

Most Internet users complain about waiting: waiting to make a connection with the ISP, waiting for a browser to load, waiting for Web sites to appear on the screen, and so on. These problems are symptoms of the rapid growth of online use and online technology. Remember that although today it's a commonplace tool, the World Wide Web was hardly known by the general public seven years ago. Picture the current situation on the information superhighway in automotive terms: Not only does the number of new cars (online computers and Web sites) on the road double every year, but all cars (new and old) double in size (graphics, audio, video) and power (interactivity) during the same year. Real roads (analogous to telephone networks and servers) would be unable to carry the traffic, and construction efforts could not keep up with the demand for more roads. It's a tribute to technology that Internet problems aren't even more common and that most users' needs are accommodated within a reasonable time.

The dedicated telephone line needed to connect to a traditional CRS transmitted data at 9,600–14,000 kilobytes per second (kbps). This speed is nowhere near sufficient to handle the graphical information of the World Wide Web. Today's requirements demand, at the very least, modems with a speed of 56,000 baud. Your needs will dictate the selection of equipment.

Bandwidth

Because there are so many more users and Web sites every day, the capacity of telephone lines and modems is being severely taxed. Fortunately, new lanes on the information superhighway are available, albeit at a price.

Interactive Television

In 1994 the cable television industry announced, with great fanfare, that it would be investing billions of dollars to bring interactive television to our homes. The plan included home shopping and video on demand. Much of this grandiose scheme fizzled because "interactive programming ... found another pipeline to the home, and that pipeline [was] the Internet."[2]

Cable Modems

Some cable television companies got on the Internet bandwagon by offering cable modems that were enormously faster than anything else available in a similar price range. "If you were downloading a file from the Internet of a picture of the Mona Lisa, it would take 1.4 hours over a telephone modem, but just 18 seconds over the cable modem."[3] In addition to vastly improved speed, a cable modem does not use a phone line, and the computer to which it is connected is always online. Modem speed and continuous access became critical as more and more audio and video features were added to the Web and as Windows-based systems became more popular.

Unfortunately, cable modems were available only in buildings that were already wired for cable television; in other words, mostly in residential areas. Until commercial areas and buildings could be hooked up to cable, homeowners had better and faster access at a smaller price than businesses.

Other Technologies

Data transmission via satellite became another option to increase bandwidth (speed). The field is still relatively open, as the demand for speed and bandwidth constantly spawns new technologies and services, as well as aggressive competition for customers.

File Transfer Protocol (FTP) is one good way to download big files (audio, databases, pictures, text, video) and to upload large files, such as new Web pages, to a server.

■ Remnants of the Early Days

While you watch the ever-changing field of telecommunications and Internet access options, you may as well learn a little about ancient Internet information sources that people used in the olden days—the early 1990s. Most people using the Internet today work within the confines of the World Wide Web. As an informed user, though, you ought to know about some other nooks and crannies that contain information. These backwaters predate the Web and are almost exclusively limited to text. Archie and Gopher resources are just two examples of Internet information formats that have, for the most part, gone extinct, though the information remains available to those who know how to find and access it.

■ Summary

Before you leap onto the Web, you need to know what you are looking for. A client database comes in handy for this purpose. Once on the Internet, you navigate with specific URLs and with search engines. You can also participate in mailing lists and look up information in non-Web areas.

The Internet is a democratic place: it gives the same information to everybody. If you want to maintain an advantage over your clients, you must learn to get to the needed information more quickly and more accurately than they can. You must also be able to judge the veracity and relevance of displayed information.

End Notes

[1] AltaVista press release, 11 February 1997.

[2] Jube Shiver, Jr., "Time Warner's Interactive TV Project Blinks," *Los Angeles Times*, 2 April 1997, D4.

[3] @Home press release, 13 July 1996.

CHAPTER 6

Disseminating Information: Selling on the Web

Chapter Outline

Objectives

After completing this chapter, you should be able to:

- Describe cybermarketing concepts
- Sell with e-mail
- Discuss push and pull marketing
- Use Web sites as selling tools
- Promote a Web site

■ Introduction

Most people using the Internet have demographic profiles that make a marketer's mouth water. High percentages of affluent, young, male, and highly educated people were the first users of the Internet. As online computing continued to expand and mature, its audience widened beyond the initial computer-expert core (see Figure 6-1).

According to the *Costco Connection* of June, 1997, there were nearly 40 million Americans surfing the Web, then nearly double the 21.5 million estimate of one year earlier. These figures came from a *Business Week* survey of 1,000 U.S. households.

- Nearly two-fifths of the 40 million surfers were women. That was up from a 1995 estimate of 23 percent.
- About a quarter of all Net users were over 40 years of age.
- About two-fifths had household incomes exceeding $50,000 a year.
- Caucasians represented about 85 percent of the online population.

FIGURE 6-1 Web doubles surfers

Research from 1998 confirmed this development. Nielsen Media Research and CommerceNet estimated in August, 1998 that "70.2 million Americans over 16 use the Internet. That represents 35 percent of adult Americans; the same study in September 1997 counted 52 million Americans online, or 26 percent." The study added that "among the fastest-growing groups online were blacks and [Native Americans], as well as young adults 16–24 and women over 50." In fact, the "study estimated [that] 40.1 million American men and 30.1 million women use the Internet, and that the percentage growth among men and women overall during the nine-months period was about the same." Consider these changes, and current trends, when developing marketing and selling strategies.

■ World Wide Web

The World Wide Web (WWW, or W3, or the Web) is still just one aspect of the Internet, but because of its capabilities it became the Internet's major component, replacing many older text-only interfaces. Once you are online with a modern browser, you'll be cruising the Web that appears on your screen complete with graphics, text, interactivity, audio, and video, depending on your computer's capabilities.

Browsers

As discussed in chapter 3, a computer must be equipped with a browser to process the information received from and sent to the Internet. Two popular browsers in the United States are Netscape Communicator and Microsoft Internet Explorer. Both products are excellent, and it is likely that your computer arrived with one or the other product already installed. Most people stick with what their machines come with.

These browsers can access information originating from just about any computer with access to the Internet. Regardless of whether information is stored in an IBM mainframe computer or on a Macintosh, the browser is able to interpret and access the information.

Web Portals

Many companies tried to provide users with a more versatile Internet starting point, complete with the latest news, weather, browsing, and searching. Cable television, Internet service providers, and search engine operators tried to hold each user's interest beyond simple searches, and for this reason they created personalized services that offered e-mail, personalized news, access to chat and newsgroups, and often a personalized home page. This combination of services made access and selection of information easier. This hot idea of 1998 is called a *Web portal*. The Web portal was supposed to be one's rent-free home on the Internet, which gave lots of service in exchange for exposing the user to its advertisers and sponsors. Aside from personal convenience, though, you need to appreciate the nature of this new medium to realize the selling potential it may hold for you.

Niche Marketing

The Internet presents you with a unique opportunity to make your travel expertise available to anybody in the world who has access to an online computer; this is an opportunity entirely novel. To translate this simple theory into practice, you'll have to do a lot of thinking and working. Before you even start to dream about Internet marketing, you need to define your specialty—but don't worry yet about profit margins and commissions. Noodle around with your concepts: What makes your professional knowledge special? How can you make it even more special? Talk to friends and associates about your abilities, ideas, and concepts, and have them ask you questions about it. Discuss your skills with colleagues at work and at school. Take their comments seriously, and use them to refine your thinking about what is unique and superior about your expertise.

For example, a former student of mine had the idea to organize a family reunion at their "ancestral" port of entry in the South. In the course of handling reservations from numerous family members, she became involved in the study of genealogy; as a result, she was able to make this family reunion more meaningful and informative than just a big backyard barbecue. She had really enjoyed making these arrangements, so she did a lot of thinking and strategizing about how to turn this unique skill set into a business. What helped her was the fact that delighted family members referred friends and business associates, who asked her to put together *their* family reunions complete with a genealogical component. Thereafter, she went to travel school to gain technical expertise that she now combines with her "people," organizational, and genealogical skills. She conducts her work from home as an outside agent, and she uses the Internet as her major tool to make travel arrangements, to stay in touch with clients, and to market her unique service.

■ The Internet Marketplace

As soon as your assessment of your unique expertise is complete, you need to think about your potential clients. What makes the Internet so useful for small travel businesses is the fact that you can potentially reach millions of people around the world on a small budget. You can reach them, you can educate them, and then you can sell them. The key to your success in cyberspace is not your technological prowess, but your ability to market your Web site and to attract clients and prospects to it. Even the most sophisticated e-mail campaign will fail if it does not elicit a good response, and even a fantastically well-designed Web site will gather virtual dust if nobody visits it. The success of your venture depends on your ability to define your market and on your knack for reaching it effectively.

Birds of a feather flock together on the Internet too, so you can use your hunting instinct to locate your target groups' online roosting areas (the sites and services they frequent). These may be Web sites or discussion groups where you can put up signposts to your services.

■ Push and Pull

Traditional electronic and print advertising is done in a "push" mode: whether or not you like an ad, a billboard, or a commercial, you have to look at it because it is being "pushed" to you. In contrast, in cyberspace people visit your site (your virtual store) because they want to have a look at it; they "pull" information in. This state of affairs, where consumers decide which ads they want to see, was completely foreign—and highly undesirable—to the traditional advertising folks. In their quest to share information with you, they brought push advertising to the Internet; you'll see advertisements in the form of banner ads on many screens.

■ E-Mail

Think of e-mail as a simple and effective method to push your message in front of clients. Despite the rumors that the Internet is a lousy sales tool (see Figure 6-2 on page 80), good e-mail marketing pays off as long as it is done professionally and consistently.

E-mail is a cheap and easy communication tool, and it has surpassed the U.S. Postal Service as the premier communications delivery system in the United States. It can replace corporate "snail" mail and expensive, time-consuming promotional faxes and mailings. E-mail increases productivity and reduces mailing costs because the expense, time, and effort needed to reach people or groups of people anywhere in the world are all low.

Free e-mail services are easily available. Most ISPs and portals offer e-mail as an included feature. A pioneering free e-mail service was Hotmail (http://www.hotmail.com/). Hotmail users accessed their e-mail from any online computer, anywhere and anytime.

Years	1996	1997	1998	1999	2000
Computer Products	$140	$ 323	$ 701	$1,228	$2,105
Travel	126	276	572	961	1,579
Entertainment	85	194	420	733	1,250
Apparel	46	89	163	234	322
Gifts and Flowers	45	103	222	386	658
Food and Drink	39	78	149	227	336
Others	37	75	144	329	329
TOTALS	$518	$1,138	$2,371	$3,990	$6,579

FIGURE 6-2 Internet's Irresistible Appeal? (in millions of $). Projected online shopping revenue (in millions of $)[1]

This feature allowed frequent travelers to stay in touch with their home bases, and it allowed agents to stay in touch with their roaming clients. With such a service, you and they are never out of touch for long; you can almost always send and receive important communications. Some of the free e-mail services include:

iName (AltaVista's e-mail)
http://www.iname.com/
Eudora Webmail
http://www.eudoramail.com/
HotMail (part of the MSN network)
http://www.hotmail.com/
LycosEmail
http://www.mail.lycos.com/
Yahoo! Mail
http://mail.yahoo.com/

E-mail is as important a business tool as the telephone. If you don't use them with the same skill, you're not using e-mail well. You'll be able to distribute valuable news and sales bulletins to your clients with ease, lightning speed, and minimal cost, and you will stay well ahead of your competitors.

One-on-One E-Mail

Suppose you find a great package tour that looks perfect for some of your clients, or a hotel special with a fast-approaching expiration date. You can make several phone calls to various clients, repeating the same message and spending time chatting with them, or you can send an identical e-mail message to each of these clients. You may do this from home or the office, or from wherever you have access to an online computer. You may even want to spruce up your message by attaching a picture or a colorful map correlating with these great travel opportunities. E-mail allows you to send an instant promotional message to your clients that they can read whenever they have the time and inclination to do so. There's no need to leave messages, and there's no danger of interrupting clients' more important business. The client can think about your offer and reply to you via e-mail. Clients can read e-mail and reply to messages from anywhere in the world, as long as they have access to an online computer.

Broadcast E-Mail

Suppose you see a great travel opportunity on the Web that looks perfect for *all* your clients, or for a large group of your clients. Many browsers have mailing-list capabilities. Get the raw material from your database and use an e-mail application to create various lists that allow you to broadcast the same message to all the people on the list at once.

By contrast, printed newsletters often constitute a real problem for travel agents. Many agents do not have the technical skills needed to publish a good-looking newsletter regularly, and well-intentioned efforts often flounder. Not so with an e-mail newsletter: this tool has to be short and its format simple. You may want to think of your e-mail newsletter as a continuing stream of information flowing from you to your potential clients, to tickle your clients' fancies.

The content and style of a broadcast message depend on the news you convey and the clientele you are addressing. See the examples shown on page 82.

You will want to create a new list of recipients for each newsletter according to its content. A good client database is an excellent tool with which to craft customized lists of e-mail addresses. You write your concise news message, possibly attach interesting files and graphics—and out it goes.

- - - - - - - - - -E-mail announcement: Airfare war - - - - - - - - - -

Subject: Lower Airfares

American Airlines has just announced fare reductions of up to 50% for a limited number of flights and seats. Call me today and let me help you save $$$ on your next trip!

Heidi at Ocean Blue Travel (123) 555-1234

- - - -E-mail announcement: Recommended new Web site - - - -

Subject: New Notable Web Site

I've been pretty good about getting regular oil changes for my cars lately. Since I registered with www.oilchange.com [a fantasy site], I get e-mail reminding me to have the oil changed. For me, this has been working better than my calendar, and my cars are much happier.

Heidi at Ocean Blue Travel (123) 555-1234

- - - - - -E-mail announcement: Message with attachment - - - - - -

Subject: Your Planned Safari to Lake Turkana

I found the attached information at softdisk.com. Because it was hard to find within an obscure Web site, I attached it for you—hope it contains the information you are looking for!

Heidi at Ocean Blue Travel (123) 555-1234

If you don't want to target your messages to specific client groups, an e-mail newsletter can be sent to all clients, as the cost of such a newsletter is minuscule. However, avoid annoying your clients with what they may regard as junk e-mail.

▧ Pulling with a Web Site

A Web site is your "open 24/7/365" store on the Internet where you vie for the interest of millions of information shoppers. Many newcomers to the Internet think that if they build a Web site, people will come. Nothing could be further from reality. You must pull them in, or you will remain hitless.

Hits

As long as you have an interesting site and promote it continuously, you may get as many hits (visits) as a site put up by a multibillion-dollar megacorporation.

It is important that you put on your thinking cap and ponder seriously to identify specifically what is unique about your agency. Merely promoting "travel service" will get you nowhere and bring you no new business; there are simply too many competitors in that undifferentiated field. Unusual and offbeat approaches have a much better chance of bringing new people into your virtual store.

Hits Lead to Sales

The art of selling on the Internet consists of getting hits and converting hits into sales. This is easier said than done. It is obvious, though, that you have to get hits before you can get sales—and you'll get hits by advertising and announcing your site wherever you can. You'll get hits by titling your Web pages intelligently. You'll get hits by having other companies and organizations provide links to your page. You already know how to get hits by selectively using broadcast e-mail as a lure. Keep your visitors engaged and interested and you'll convert hits into sales.

Signposts

Locate signposts pointing to your agency at popular Internet meeting places. Your CRS's Web site is such a place, and so are real and virtual community sites.

Outside Links

Work with other companies and organizations for cross-fertilization. For example, let's suppose that you want to promote your special wine-tasting tour of France on your Web site. You first need to find out which wineries, cities, and hotels featured in your tour have their own Web sites. Then you contact these companies and organizations and tell them about your promotion and ask them to create links to your French wine tour page. Of course, you also remind them that you are creating links to their sites, too. Such links can be very productive and they are usually provided free of charge.

As another example, suppose you send a group of wildlife biologists to an international conference in Australia. In this case, you should look up all the sites that have to do with wildlife biology to see where you could put up signposts to your trip.

You can also ask local businesses, clubs, and organizations to provide a link to your company. This is networking on the Internet level. Looking for such contacts is easy with the help of a search engine.

Links from your Web site to other sites may lead your visitors astray, though: Surfers may wander from one site to the next and never return to your site. You may also point your visitors to links that have gone stale or dead—and visitors hate it when that happens! Despite these perils, good outside links make your Web site more attractive and informative, and reciprocal links are essential to maintain traffic.

■ Web Page Titles

Each Web page has a title. Although these titles do not necessarily appear on viewers' screens, they are of utmost importance. More than anything else, they are most likely to be noticed by the Web crawlers and spiders that feed the voracious search engines. Further discussion of Web pages will follow in chapter 7.

■ Summary

You do not need a Web site to use the Internet as a marketing tool. CRS services help agencies establish a presence on the Internet. However, when you build a Web site, present your agency as a unique business, and make sure Web crawlers and spiders know about it.

End Notes

[1] Forrester Research, Inc., quoted in Jared Sandberg, "Making the Sale," *Wall Street Journal,* 17 June 1996, R6.

CHAPTER 7

The Web Coordinator: Creating, Updating, and Monitoring a Web Site

Chapter Outline

Objectives

After completing this chapter, you should be able to:

- Detail the need for and uses of a Web site
- Develop a Web site philosophy
- Discuss Web site design considerations

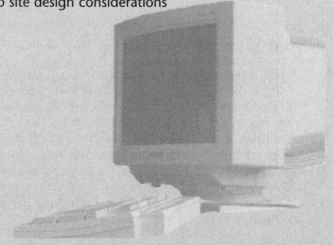

■ The Web Coordinator

Everyone needs to know how to use the Internet to send and receive e-mail and to find information. In contrast, the tasks of creating, updating, and monitoring commercial Web sites take specialized skills and are usually carried out by Web coordinators. Responsibility for the Web site should be clearly assigned to a Web-savvy individual in the agency. The Web coordinator should be a staff member who is well versed in both the retail travel business and online technology. A good on-staff (preferably in-house) Web coordinator is essential to keep a site's content accurate and current. Offsite solutions tend to lead to inaccuracies and slow site updates.

Web coordinators deal with outside Web-related matters (servers, consultants, CRS services), produce site style guides, keep the site up to date, upload edited and new pages to the server, and obtain traffic reports. Web coordinators who can create and write highly sophisticated pages and pull together entire Web sites, and who can handle an onsite server, are typically referred to as *Webmasters*. Visiting http://www.clickz.com keeps Web coordinators well informed.

All new entrants into the travel industry need to be conversant with Web site content and design considerations, because Web sites will become a centerpiece of agency life. Agency managers need to be familiar with the subject matter so they can give direction to the Web coordinator; agents need to be involved in the process, too, because the Web site can be truly effective only with their input. For these reasons, the following discussion is not aimed only at the technologically advanced—each agent should be aware of all these considerations.

■ A View of the Future

REI (Recreational Equipment Incorporated), headquartered in Sumner, Washington, has a fine Web site (http://www.rei.com) where the company provides excellent information about its products and where it increasingly sells them, too. To spread similar information throughout the company, REI tested online computers in lieu of cash registers; online kiosks were installed in many of its stores. This expanded access to the company's Web site was designed to enable sales clerks to provide customers with information about any aspect of the store, including inventory, out-of-stock products, travel services, and so on. In addition, employees could access client profiles, such as past purchases, and thus suggest appropriate new products without having to ask repetitive questions. This function was to be automated over time, much as amazon.com automated book recommendations for established customers. The apparent oddity of REI's approach was that in-store access to the Web provided live customers with as much information as virtual visitors.

As shown by the REI example, the Web has invaded every aspect of every business, with innovative new uses springing up constantly. It should be obvious that at least some knowledge of Web site creation and management is becoming essential.

■ Selling: One Step at a Time

You have come to appreciate the sudden emergence of the Internet as a major force in commerce and perhaps in our entire culture. You have learned to collect information on the Internet, and you have learned to communicate using e-mail. However, some people estimate that between 30,000 and 50,000 pages are added to the Web every day, so consider this warning from the president of CDnow Inc. before you decide to set up your own Web site: "There are a lot of people out there who are developing online presences because they feel they have to, and not because they have justification." He also noted that "selling is a reason to bother with the Web. Marketing isn't."[1] The following sections will help you consider the advantages and disadvantages of operating your own Web site, and learn what it takes to operate a Web site—your virtual store/office that is open around the clock to the entire world.

Previous chapters explored the changing travel marketplace and discussed some ideas on how to adapt to it and make it work for you. The concepts covered previously—including entrepreneurial thinking, niche marketing, and aggressive selling—can work only if you can offer something that your clients consider unique. The earlier chapters also emphasized that the Internet reduces the value of physical proximity to clients as a unique asset.

E-Mail Marketing, the Simplest Approach

Many agencies and agents consider the relationships with their clients to be a unique asset, and location may be part of this relationship. Therefore, anything that can strengthen these ties should be considered. E-mail marketing, as discussed in chapter 6, may be the way to keep online clients from straying to big online agencies. This approach does *not* require a Web site.

An Off-the-Shelf Web Site

The CRS services offered Web sites to their agents at no or low cost, as discussed in chapter 2. With the combination of e-mail selling and a CRS-built virtual Web site, your online customers can use your Web site to research travel plans and make reservations. Small or home-based business clients may especially appreciate your simple Web site.

This is an easy step into the online environment. First, it tells your online clients that you're moving with the flow. More importantly, you give them the opportunity to use the Web's travel potential without abandoning your agency. Last but not least, this technique requires only minimal input from you.

A Custom Web Site

Keeping up with the Internet and the World Wide Web is a continuous process. Ten years ago, few people even knew about the existence of the World Wide Web, yet today it has become commonplace.

Using e-mail and a virtual CRS Web site may very well fulfill your agency's online needs, but you may find that to provide your clients with information about products only your agency offers, you need a custom Web site. A custom Web site can help you sell and promote:

- Group departures (tours, cruises, and other packages)
- Unique travel programs (incoming and outgoing)
- Discounted programs
- Coupons
- Last minute specials

Selling on the Web is not much different from traditional travel selling, inasmuch as both use essentially soft-sell techniques. Plenty of information must be given to a potential client before a sale is made. The beauty of a Web site is that it hands out this information and advice automatically and around the clock. For a Web site to become an effective part of an agency's sales and marketing efforts, careful consideration must be given to site form and content.

■ Web Site Form and Content

You must know precisely what you are selling before you can start thinking about the contents and location of your Web site. You must have a clear idea of how your agency is different from others, and how its strengths benefit clients. Because the Internet is information driven, you'll have to spell out your unique selling proposition on your Web site.

A Web site must be fully integrated into an agency's structure. Thus, general knowledge of Web site management is a must for anybody in charge of such a business.

Content Considerations

A consultant cannot help you figure out what the best content for your Web site is. Only you know what attracts, interests, and is useful to your clients. Only you know what has been selling profitably and repeatedly. Only you know the unique strengths of your services, your staff, your location, and your contacts. Only you know what price advantages you can offer. Simply put, only you can establish the content of your Web site. This section helps you organize that content.

Web Site Musts

Although the Web is a chaotic and dynamic place, some key features simply must be part of a good Web site, regardless of that site's content. It is important for the people who are dealing with and deciding on Web page content and design to look outside their specific industries often, to remain informed about what's new and what's hot. Some of the following considerations and factors may not apply to your situation, but most of them will.

Vital Links

Links to pages that show "What's New," "Where We Are," and "Who We Are" must appear in one form or another on your home page, preferably in your navigational top bar. The main benefit of a "What's New" feature is that it prompts visitors to return to your page to check out changes. Consequently, this feature (page) must be updated regularly, and its design ought to be simple so that it can be edited easily by agency staff. The "Where We Are" section tells visitors about the agency or agent's location (with a map), hours of operation, telephone and fax numbers, and so on. Finally, the "Who We Are" page talks about the agency's philosophy, its management, and its staff. Photographs and chatty copy are perfect for this section.

Navigation

Navigational tools help visitors find where they want to go within your site. If they cannot quickly find what they are looking for, they will look elsewhere. Often, a navigational top bar meets this requirement (see Figure 7-1).

FIGURE 7-1 A navigational top bar from **http://www.mtsobek.com**
(Courtesy of Mountain Travel—Sobek, El Cerrito, CA)

Interactivity

Make it easy for visitors to get in touch with you. References to your guest book and opportunities to send e-mail to individual staff members ought to be sprinkled liberally throughout the site.

Simple, Consistent Design

Display your navigational tool(s) on each page and keep the design simple and user-friendly. Place your company's name, address, telephone and fax numbers, e-mail addresses, and Web URLs on each page—remember, visitors may first reach one of your sub-pages instead of your home page. Therefore, a "Home" link (leading back to your home page) must be part of every page, too. Although animated elements can be cute, they tend to increase download time, clutter up a page, and distract your visitors' attention from your message.

Privacy and Security

Unless you publish your privacy policy, visitors may be unwilling even to consider leaving their names and addresses in your guest book. Be honest and upfront: tell them what you plan to do with the information you receive from them, and provide them with complete information about your security protocols for financial transactions. This, of course, means that you must *have* security protocols in place—and they must be as good as you can possibly get if you intend to conduct financial transactions over the Internet. Many consumers are (justifiably) still quite reluctant to reveal any personal or financial information on the Internet.

Offsite Links

Consider including a list of links to sites that might be of interest to your clients, such as the U.S. State Department's and the Centers for Disease Control's travel advisories.

Behind the Screen

Responsibility for the Web site should be clearly assigned to an individual in the agency, the Web coordinator. Even if he or she does not do the initial Web design, this person is usually tasked with maintaining the site, updating it, monitoring use, and troubleshooting any problems that arise.

■ Design Considerations

Market research is essential before you even begin designing your site. The best look and content for your Web site are what intrigues, attracts, and serves your clients. Find out what kind of computer equipment most of your clients use, and avoid advanced features that your clients cannot handle or take advantage of. Be aware of your clients' demographics: You don't want to fashion your Web site in a way that shocks or offends clients, or clashes with their lifestyle. Beware of Web page designs that dazzle with the latest special effects. At best, those amazing effects may distract your site visitors; at worst, they may not display properly on users' screens and may take forever to download. If clients have to wait too long—more than about 15 seconds!—for a Web page to display, they'll be gone before it appears. Professional Web site designers use the latest equipment and are often infatuated with frames, sound, Java, XML, and other wonderful, newfangled techniques that may not work for your clients. Know your market and know what you're selling; then make sure the site designer presents your message appropriately.

You have already visited many Web sites and you have a good idea of what you like and what you don't, of what works on your screen and what doesn't. You have seen sites that wowed you and others that bored you. You may have been overwhelmed by glitzy, flashy, tricky sites, or you may have been impressed with a conservative but well-executed approach. Remember that a successful site must astound, inform, and entertain your *clients,* not you and not your Web page consultant. Decide which general presentation style is best suited to your clientele. Use a look that will appeal to your clients.

To work well on your clients' computers, your Web site must be written in a language that can be deciphered by the majority of your clients' browsers. Unfortunately, there is still precious little standardization in this area. Each new browser performs more tricks than its predecessor, but Web site developers must be careful not to load a site with too many new features that older browsers cannot recognize or display. Many sites offer special pages with a low graphic content or text-only content for users with older browsers and/or slow modems. Depending on your business's clientele, this is a technique to consider.

Users' Attention Span

Surfing the Internet is often much like channel surfing on television. You stop when you come upon an interesting, arresting scene; you move on when something is not of interest to you. Your Web site's home page (your opening page) must cause the casual viewer to stop and look. What's more, your pages must not only halt the viewers' click-throughs while they digest your presentation, but they must also cause these users to click on your links. A good home page draws in clients just as a good store window display draws customers into a store.

Essential Design Elements

You get attention with three design elements that must be present on every page of your site:

1. Headlines and concise text
2. Graphics
3. Links

These elements are particularly important on your home page. Keep in mind that many visitors are casual browsers, and you must capture their attention very quickly. Be sure your home page loads within a few seconds; many visitors will click on the Stop button if they have to wait longer than 10 seconds for a page to load onto their screens.

Embed these three design elements in an open, consistent overall design that continues throughout your site's pages. Don't crowd the screen with too much material—less is more! When you have a lot to say, break it down into a multipage presentation (see Figure 7-2).

FIGURE 7-2 A sample home page from **http://www.kahalatravel.com/** (Courtesy of Kahala Travel, San Diego, CA)

Text

Writing copy for the Web differs from other writing because of the Web's unique technology: The Web is nonlinear, interactive, and very graphic-oriented. It's also an informal place where brisk and pithy language succeeds better than wordy, complicated text.

Web site visitors are used to jumping all over the place with links. They tend not to read a document from top to bottom, and they tend to follow links until they find precisely what they want. Large chunks of plain text are boring, look awful on the screen, force viewers to scroll, and often drive them away.

Engage visitors in interactivity by asking questions and conducting surveys and contests.

Replace text with graphics whenever possible.

You have some choices as to the font, or type style, of the letters that will appear on your visitors' screens. The written characters are created by each browser and are standard, but you can select the size of a font and the placement of words and lines on the screen.

Headlines

Organize text neatly by using headlines. These headlines instantly impart a visual structure to your page. Your text has to be short and viewer-oriented: Address visitors with "you" and be casual but respectful. Present lists with links and complement them with graphics whenever possible. It's usually a bad idea to turn a brochure into a Web page, because printed information is usually verbose, linear (you read from beginning to end), and passive (there are neither links nor fill-in forms).

Links

A Web page without links is like an action movie without sound. Links and graphics bring pizzazz to your pages. You can create text links easily, and viewers spot them quickly. The screen usually shows text links in blue letters that are underlined. This tells viewers that a "wormhole" to another world exists right there. There's no telling which routes viewers will take, but you can nudge them in the right direction—toward interactivity—by designing with the viewer in mind.

Cater to Wandering Eyes

After Gutenberg ushered in the printed book with his invention of movable type in the 15th century, it took more than 100 years for organizational concepts to become standardized. Chapter headings, indexes, pagination, and so on were wildly different or entirely missing in early printed books. It is the same now with the Web: It will take time for standards to develop. However, you can follow a few "universal" design concepts that have been shaped by Western traditions of reading and manuscript production. For example, text in English is read from left to right across the page and from top to bottom. Principal graphics tend to be in the upper left area or centered at the top of a page. There is nothing sacred about these conventions; it's just the way tradition has shaped readers' (and Web site viewers') expectations.

Nevertheless, you will get a better response and cause much less confusion and irritation if you allow viewers' eyes to do what they are used to doing: wandering from top left to bottom right. Let the information flow from important, attention-grabbing items at the upper left or top of the page to the less riveting items toward the center and the lower right of the page.

Graphics

Your company logo may be the most obvious graphic element of your page, but it may also leave your viewers cold. Don't abandon your logo, but don't let it dominate your design. Other design elements, such as maps and travel pictures, are probably more exciting for your visitors. Use pictures that involve and stimulate the viewer.

Background

Support the general atmosphere of your Web site with an appropriate background. When you look at other pages, pay close attention to how the background color and texture create a mood. A vast selection of background graphics is available. In fact, with so many nifty designs, you may be tempted to use a whole smorgasbord of backgrounds and colors in your site. Resist this temptation! Instead, aim to establish a consistent design throughout your Web pages, and stick to the same general layout and background as much as possible.

▓ Vital Data and Consistent Design

Make it easy for your viewers to know whose page they are visiting by giving your company name and a link back to the home page on every page, in the same place on each page. If your agency provides assistance in foreign languages, you may want to add pictures of flags as links to your foreign-language pages; be consistent with the placement of these graphics. If your agency specializes in travel for the handicapped, you may want to add a picture of a wheelchair as a link to your handicapped travelers' information page; again, be consistent with the placement of these graphics.

When you visit Web design sites, you'll see many attention-grabbing elements that could enliven or jazz up your pages. You might be tempted by a flashing, red burst indicating your best sellers; you might fall in love with an animated mail box that invites people to send you e-mail; you might want to punch up your bulleted lists with bullets that are full-color turning globes. A word of caution, though: When using other people's work (graphics, photos, text), you must respect the copyright laws, or you may find yourself in very serious trouble.

You have undoubtedly seen pages that are chock-a-block with graphic gismos that blink and move and streak across the screen. Be cautious and use such special effects judiciously! Your Web site has to appeal to your clients for its content and ease of use, not as a testimonial to your imagination and design prowess. Furthermore, large or complicated graphics almost always significantly reduce the speed at which your pages appear on visitors' screens.

A consistent look to and organization of your Web pages are most important in supporting the content of your site. Your visitors ought to feel stimulated by your information, and you want them to feel comfortable visiting and using your site. A congenial and constant design appropriate for your audience is mandatory.

Essentials

Regardless of the organization and design of a travel agency Web site, some essential areas simply have to be included on the home page:

- Complete agency information
- Link to reservations page, area, or facility
- Link to last-minute deals (specials)
- Link to agency specialty (for example, Hawaii packages)
- Link to an "About Our Agency" page or section
- Links to e-mail for the agency in general and for specific agents
- Copyright information

More on Links

Links are endemic to the Web for good reason: They add depth and pizzazz to your pages, they make this medium truly different and exciting, and they are useful. Links allow the visitor to jump from page to page and from site to site. For example, a viewer could click on "Hawaii" and be transported instantly to your Hawaii page, where you give more specific information about your Hawaii tours. Your Hawaii main page would have yet more links to more detailed information about hotels, specific islands, departure dates, included services, and so forth. Figure 7-3 shows how a Web site might be organized.

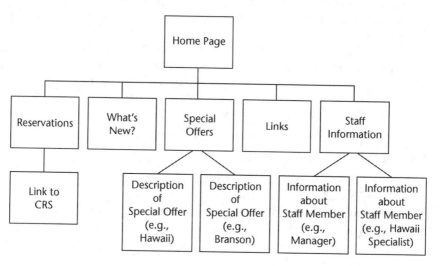

FIGURE 7-3 Diagram of Web site organization

Links can also allow your visitors to jump to an altogether different site. Continuing the previous example, you might want to have a link to the Hawaii Tourist Council pages, where your visitors can find a treasure trove of information. When you provide external links, be sure to recheck the URLs periodically, as sites may change or disappear. Cyber travelers hate to be led to dead sites. You also want to make sure that your links don't lead to your competitors' Web sites!

Interactivity

Engage your visitors in fun and meaningful activities and games. A simple example of interactivity is an e-mail address linked to a fill-in form, so that—upon completion—the form is automatically and immediately forwarded from the client to your e-mail address. Forms are a good way to draw in clients and to expand your client database with very little effort.

Here's another example: Within your cruise page selection, you could offer some cruise jokes and invite visitors to contribute their own. You might invite your visitors to enter a contest for one of your travel products, or you could set up a "Travel Quiz of the Month."

Remember, by sending you messages, visitors reveal their e-mail addresses, which you can add to your mailing list (database). It is important that you state your privacy policy whenever you invite a visitor to leave his or her URL with you. Be honest and tell your visitors what you intend to do with their addresses.

It's unlikely that visitors will sign up for a trip without making a phone call or contacting you directly. Aim your entire Web site, and especially its interactive features, toward the more casual visitors, and invite them to come in. Once they are comfortable with you, they'll be ready to buy.

Freshness

You need to keep your site fresh and updated. A page devoted to "What's New" must be attended to constantly. Design this page so that it can be updated with a minimum of cost and fuss.

■ Summary

A simple Web site, like those offered by most CRS services, is a must for every travel agency. Know what you are selling, and to whom, before you think of starting your own Web site. Establish content and form yourself—an Internet business consultant cannot do this for you! Form follows content on Web pages, too. Tailor content and design to the taste of your clientele; include the three basic design elements on each page, and keep your site up to date.

End Notes

[1] Quoted in Jared Sandberg, "Making the Sale," *Wall Street Journal*, 17 June 1996, R6.

CHAPTER 8

Web Site Management and Windows Systems

Chapter Outline

Web Authoring Software

Why Learn HTML?

Modifying a Web Page

Writing a Web Page

Announcing Your Web Site to the World

Web Site Analysis

Microsoft Windows Systems and Applications

Objectives

After completing this chapter, you should be able to:

- Identify the functions and capabilities of Web authoring software
- Discuss the use of HTML for creating Web pages
- Understand what goes on behind the scenes of Web sites

Web Authoring Software

Web page designers used to laboriously write pages and pages of code in HTML, which stands for HyperText Markup Language. Now, just as CRS code knowledge is less important because of easy point-and-click reservation screens, HTML code knowledge is less crucial because of Web authoring software that automatically writes the code. Among the most popular Web authoring tools are Microsoft's FrontPage and its simpler version, FrontPage Express, though many professional designers use other, more sophisticated tools. This section discusses some features of FrontPage and similar programs and then looks into some reasons why code knowledge may still be required for those who create and update custom Web sites.

With FrontPage or FrontPage Express, even novices can create entire Web sites. Excellent FrontPage tutorials can be found online, and many community colleges and trade schools teach the use of this program and others like it. Although many will want to take a class before they attempt the task, more advanced users may be able to jump right into using these programs.

Why Learn HTML?

Reading and writing in HTML are important skills for anybody who wants to understand, develop, monitor, and maintain sophisticated Web pages and sites. Reading/writing in HTML is called *working with the source code*. Luckily, travel agents are used to code, because any CRS requires knowledge of some codes. Musicians know another code: music notation. As they read it, good musicians "hear" the music; you may get to the point where you can read HTML and "see" the Web pages in your mind.

Think of HTML as the grammar of Web page design. You don't need French grammar to ask for the nearest restaurant in Paris or Quebec; however, if you want to move beyond simple French phrases, a basic understanding of grammar concepts and a fundamental vocabulary are essential. Those who depend on electronic translators and phrase books will not be able to advance to real conversation and understanding of a language. Likewise, those who depend entirely on the use of HTML editors and automatic authoring programs will have a hard time reading and writing code. These aids are helpful and useful, but they do not eliminate the need for a basic understanding of code writing. That's why HTML knowledge is important for Web coordinators and Webmasters.

Although you certainly could not consider yourself an accomplished French speaker with only a vocabulary of a few dozen words and knowledge of some grammar rules, you could probably understand basic information given to you in French. The goal in Web page authoring is similar: You learn the features of a HTML editor, become familiar with its capabilities and limitations, and then you learn some of the basic concepts of HTML. In the process you learn to modify and create a simple Web page with the help of an editor and with the help of HTML code. *Note:* Because excellent online tutorials and classes are easily available, this book does not cover even generic information about these skills.

Human languages evolve slowly, and even small changes can take hundreds of years to occur. By contrast, computer programming languages develop at a torrid pace. During its relatively short life span, HTML has changed and expanded ceaselessly. HTML evolved through improvements and changes such as Javascript, Dynamic HTML, and XML (Expanded Markup Language). An altogether new language arose with JAVA. All of these valuable innovations go beyond the purview of this book, but keen agents may want to add one or more of these enhancements to their tool kits and skills. This advice is especially directed to agents who are more interested in developing travel Web sites than in selling travel services.

Finally, Microsoft's Windows systems brought HTML into the realm of word processing. The Windows operating system, in concert with MS Word, encouraged the creation of documents with HTML tags. When e-mailed as attachments, these documents can be as fully interactive as Web pages.

▓ Modifying a Web Page

Most travel agencies turn to professional Web site designers to create and design the agency's pages. Professionals usually suggest that at least one page of an agency's site be devoted to special offers, and remind the Web site owner that this page and certain other areas should be updated often to remain current and retain viewer interest.

External Links

Check external links at least once a month to see whether the pages to which they refer still exist and still do what you want them to do. It's also possible that the page still exists but now has a different URL.

What's New, Quizzes, and Staff Announcements

The dynamic areas of your site—"What's New," quiz and contest pages, time-limited offers and events, and staff pages—are worth the price of admission to your visitors and are intended to cause them to revisit frequently. It behooves you to keep them fresh and up-to-date, lest repeat visitors get bored and become former visitors.

Seasonal Graphics

Just as you change your display window in accordance with the seasons, you should add seasonal spark to your site. There are many sources where you can find appropriate backgrounds and other graphics, such as gobbling turkeys, jingling bells, popping champagne bottles, hatching Easter eggs, and fluttering flags. When used sparingly, seasonal designs add a nice touch to your pages, but do not let them go stale. Turkeys on Valentine's Day gobble of a neglected Web site.

Such updates can be taken care of by the designer or, more efficiently and at less cost, by the agency Web coordinator. An example of what is involved comes from a Cardinal Travel page with specials, found at **http://www.gocardinal.com/cruise_ honeymoon.htm** (see Figure 8-1).

Obviously, the content of this page has to be changed often to remain current. To do this, the page has to be downloaded and then edited with an HTML editor. A simple HTML editor allows the Web coordinator to change any part of the page. After the changes have been made, the updated page is saved and uploaded to the server again.

There are instances in which a simple editor such as FrontPage Express cannot handle the changes that have to be made, and the Web coordinator needs to change the actual code. This is when specialized knowledge of HTML is necessary. An extensive list and explanation of common HTML codes can be found at **http:// www.frc.ri.cmu.edu/~mcm/tags.html**. HTML coding is taught at many schools, and the examples on page 104 are just two of the many tutorials available online.

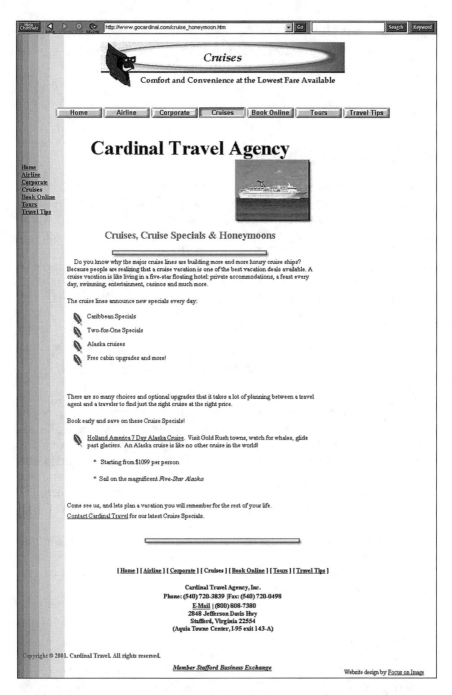

FIGURE 8-1 Cardinal Travel specials (Courtesy of Cardinal Travel Agency, Inc., Stafford, VA)

A Beginners Guide to HTML

http://archive.ncsa.uiuc.edu/General/Internet/WWW/
HTMLPrimerAll.html

Basic HTML

http://www.geocities.com/jhaslam2002/code.html

Writing a Web Page

HTML editors such as FrontPage Express make it easy to set up a page or site from scratch. However, the quality of homemade pages does not compare with that of professionally designed material. It is therefore important to distinguish between creating and designing a Web page all the way, on the one hand; and turning design and content specifications over to a Web page designer, on the other. The cost of a professional is not negligible, but your Web site, as your primary marketing and sales tool, is worth the investment to get it done well.

Announcing Your Web Site to the World

Most visitors will come to your site through a search engine. It is therefore vital that everything you do be noted by search engines. As discussed earlier, search engines send out robots to ferret out information about each Web page, and they usually use the title sections and/or the top few lines of Web pages for indexing. Keep in mind that it takes search-engine robots between one (AltaVista, Infoseek) and eight (Yahoo) weeks to make a complete collection sweep of the Web—despite the fact that the Web changes every day!

By contrast, directories will not list your site unless you register it. Most ISPs do this for you for a fee. If your ISP does not, you will have to get, complete, and submit the registration forms of the various directory services yourself.

Web Site Analysis

Once a Web site is up and running, it is important to check regularly on its use by collecting use statistics and doing data analysis. Knowing who is visiting a site is important if you are to develop ever-better content and design to attract a growing audience, or to add products that better fit your actual audience. Farther down the road, user data may also be important to attract advertisers and to judge whether your hardware is keeping pace with your growth and current needs.

Most Web servers generate log files that include IP addresses of visitors, date and time stamps, files accessed, where the visitor came from (HTTP referrer), and the type of browser used. The traffic is best counted by page views or page deliveries representing the number of times a Web page is requested.

Here's what a monthly traffic report about your site may contain and what you can learn from it:

1. *Access for each day and hour of day:* Tells which days and hours of the day experience the highest use. Over time, you'll see patterns develop that you may be able to exploit.

2. *Access of each file:* Shows which pages are the most popular. In other words, here's where you find out what visitors are looking for.

3. *Access by top-level domain:* Shows where your visitors are from. This result may reveal that you have many visitors from a particular foreign country (e.g., ca [Canada]) or from universities (e.g., edu).

4. *Access by second-level domain:* Shows which kind of organization visitors use to come to you (e.g., AOL).

5. *Access by host and by full URL:* Shows from within which sites visitors found the link to your page (typically search engines).

6. *Types of browser software used by visitors:* This information could help you fine-tune your Web page design so that it displays quickly and nicely on the browsers most used to access your site.

More sophisticated and expensive analyses are offered by many Internet service providers.

■ Microsoft Windows Systems and Applications

Throughout this book are references to the many parts of the online world: from e-mail to surfing the Internet, from CRS services to Web page creation. Microsoft's Windows operating system and a selection of complementary applications can tie these pieces together so that you can serve your clients efficiently. Windows' market dominance makes familiarity with it compulsory. Although there are competing operating systems (notably Apple and Linux), they remain far behind Windows in numbers of users. The vast majority of your Web site visitors and clients will be using either Microsoft Windows-based or Apple machines.

The hallmark of Windows is the seamless integration of online and offline tasks achieved by weaving Microsoft's browser, Internet Explorer, into the very fabric of the operating system. This bundling (among other things) led to the United States government's lawsuit against Microsoft for antitrust violations. One of the results of this legal action was that Microsoft enabled Windows users to easily include and use other browsers, such as Netscape. Regardless of the legal issues, Windows made the Internet a natural and integral part of many personal computer operations. According to Microsoft, this integration shows up in a number of ways in the Windows systems:

- You can get to the Internet from any window, even from the task bar.

- You can subscribe to important Web sites and instruct the program to notify you when updates occur.

- You can browse your computer contents the same way you surf the Web.

- Using the e-mail programs Outlook and Outlook Express, you can send and receive HTML messages instead of plain text, so your messages look and act like Web pages (complete with links and text formatting).

- You can automate maintenance and updating of the program so that these tasks take place during off hours.

Windows systems also automatically detect most new peripheral devices and install the necessary drivers, particularly for devices that use Universal Serial Bus (USB) ports.

Other Microsoft products are, of course, designed to run well with Windows systems. Among the applications agents may find useful are dictionaries, thesauruses, quotation dictionaries, almanacs, atlases, and Zip Code finders. Atlases can be put to particularly good use by agents: They display location maps and information about countries and cities, and some render an audio version of the correct pronunciation of place names. References on CD are a good and convenient supplement to the information available on the Internet and the World Wide Web.

Microsoft Works or Office may meet most agents' word-processing, database, and spreadsheet needs. Microsoft Word is a complete word processor that also allows users to create documents for use on an intranet or on the Web. As mentioned, FrontPage Express is a simple HTML editor that uses "wizards" to help you create and upload Web pages.

Because Windows and many of its applications involve the Internet energetically, Internet access is critical. A narrow-band 56K modem with dial-up access may suffice, but only greater speed and continuous access fully unleash the potential of this operating system. The need for equipment or connection upgrades to broadband will become obvious as you work more and more on and through the Internet—but you can always wait until you really need them.

With Windows 98, Microsoft said goodbye to generations of the venerable MS-DOS which first saw the light of day as IBM's PC-DOS 1.0 in 1981. It was the last Windows program to have DOS as its inmost layer (kernel). Newer Windows operating systems run on the NT kernel.

The first NT Windows version, Windows NT 5, offered some features of special interest to travel agents and their suppliers. Foremost among them was the IntelliMirror, which let administrators (possibly CRS services and other vendors) load entire applications to users (travel agents) over the Internet. When the user ran the program for the first time, it installed itself automatically.

The administrator could establish the user's desktop configuration and delineate possible actions, and could make sure that only its desktop screen was used. This technology enabled CRS services to distribute their services securely and simply via the Internet.

■ Summary

The developments in computer hardware and software suggest that the conditions are ripe for a new model of the retail travel business to emerge. It will fit into the multitasking online environment, and it will be a place where powerful online computers are used to collect information and run applications simultaneously to create and sell travel services. You can be in the forefront of this exciting development!

Appendix A

Selected Web Sites

This list makes no claims either to completeness or to correctness; it has accreted over a number of years, and Web sites change daily. The purpose of this list is simply to provide some possible starting points for where you need or want to go on the Web.

Adventure travel
Http://mtsobek.com/
Http://www.abercrombiekent.com/

Adventure travel magazine
Http://highonadventure.com/

Airline and flight information
Http://www.itn.net/cgi/get?itn/pl/amex_personal/index

Flight delay reports
Http://weather.com

Frequent flyer information
Http://insideflyer.com

Lowest airfares
Http://onetravel.com/

Official Airline Guide
Http://oag.com

Air Canada
Http://aircanada.ca/

Alaska Airlines
Http://alaska-air.com/

American Airlines
Http://americanair.com/

American Airlines: special offers
http://americanair.com/apps/netSAAver/
NetSAAverHome.jhtml

British Airways
http://british-airways.com/

British Midland
http://www.flybmi.com

Delta
http://www.delta.com/

Easy Jet
http://www.easyjet.com

El Al
http://elal.co.il/

Hawaiian Airlines
http://hawaiianair.com/

Iceland Air
http://www.icelandair.com

KLM
http://www.klm.com/

LTU Airways
http://www.ltu-airways.com/

Lufthansa
http://lufthansa.com/

Mexicana
http://www.mexicana.com/

Southwest
http://iflyswa.com/

United
http://www.ual.com/

Virgin Atlantic Airways
  http://www.virgin-atlantic.com/

American Society of Travel Agents
  http://astanet.com/

Auctions

Directory of auction sites
  http://www.usaweb.com/

Car rentals

Rental car companies listed
  http://dir.yahoo.com/Business_and_Economy/Shopping_and_
  Services/Automotive/Rentals/

Advantage Rent-a-Car
  http://www.arac.com/

Alamo Rent-a-Car
  http://alamo.com/

Auto Europe
  http://www.autoeurope.com/index.cfm

Avis
  https://www.avis.com/AvisWeb/home/AvisHome

Budget
  https://rent.drivebudget.com/Home.jsp

Dollar Rent-a-Car
  http://www.dollarcar.com/

Enterprise Rent-a-Car
  http://www.enterprise.com/index.jhtml

Hertz
  http://www.hertz.com/servlet/LoginServlet

Kemwell
  http://www.kemwel.com/

National
  http://www.nationalcar.com/servlet/DocHandler/
  index.html?2e1b456787e2fd72

Payless Car Rental
  http://www.paylesscarrental.com/index.html

Rent-A-Wreck
  http://www.rent-a-wreck.com/

Sixt
  http://www.e-sixt.de/

Thrifty
  http://www.thrifty.com/

Careers and job hunting
  http://www.jobweb.com/
  http://www.shop4jobs.com/
  http://www.careerdatabase.com/

Occupational Outlook Handbook
  http://www.bls.gov/oco/

ProTravel Personnel
  http://www.traveljobsnow.com/Career_Seekers/
  findcareer.asp

Commerce on the Internet
  http://www.cio.com/research/ec/
  http://ecommerce.internet.com/
  http://www.commerce.net/

Electronic Commerce Journal
  http://www.electronicmarkets.org/

Computers

Apple/Macintosh
  http://www.apple.com/

Magazines
  http://www.cnet.com/
  http://www.computeruser.com/

Microsoft
　http://microsoft.com/ms.htm

Online backups
　http://atbackup.com
　http://www.sgii.com/

Sales
　http://www.bestbuy.com/
　http://www.compusa.com/
　http://www.pricewatch.com/
　http://www.radioshack.com/

Software
　http://www.macromedia.com/
　http://www.microsoft.com/frontpage/
　http://shareware.cnet.com/

group travel, meetings, etc.
　http://ddninc.com

telephony
　http://www.pulver.com/
　http://vocaltec.com/
　http://www.von.com/

voice recognition/talking to computer
　http://www.dragonsys.com/
　http://www-3.ibm.com/software/

CRSs

Amadeus
　http://www.us.amadeus.com/

Galileo (Apollo)
　http://www.galileo.com

Sabre
　http://www.sabre.com/

Worldspan
http://worldspan.com/map/init_index.asp

Cruise information

Agencies
http://www.cruisesofvalue.com/
http://www.cruiseshopping.com/

Carnival Cruise Lines
http://www.carnival.com/

CLIA
http://www.cruising.org/index0.htm

Clipper Cruise Lines
http://www.clippercruise.com/

Cunard
http://www.cunardline.com/index.cfm

Majesty Cruise Line
http://www.majestycruise.com/index.asp?cat=6598

Maris Freighter Cruises
http://freightercruises.com/

Norwegian Cruise Lines
http://www.ncl.com/

Royal Caribbean
http://www.royalcaribbean.com/asp/default.asp

Windstar Cruises
http://www.windstarcruises.com/

Destinations, places, and resorts

Alaska, Glacier Bay
http://www.glacierbaytours.com/

Andes (South America)
http://andes.org/

Austria
http://www.austria-tourism.at/us

California, Baja
http://www.baja.com/
http://www.bajabound.com/
http://www.bajalife.com/

Canada
http://www.arctic-travel.com/

Cayman Islands
http://silvanaus.com

China
http://www.chinavoyages.com/

Club Mediterranee
http://www.clubmed.com/

Egypt, Great Pyramid at Giza
http://www.pbs.org/wgbh/nova/pyramid/

Florida, Miami Beach
http://www.miamiandbeaches.com/

France, Paris
http://www.geocities.com/Paris/3554/
http://www.parisparis.com/
http://www.smartweb.fr/

Germany
http://www.germany-tourism.de/

Hawaii
http://www.gohawaii.com/
http://www.hshawaii.com/

Hawaii, Kauai
http://www.kauai-hawaii.com/

Hawaii, Maui
http://www.islandcurrents.com/

Israel
http://www.israeltour.com/

Italy
http://www.italiantourism.com
http://www.monterosa.com/

Japan (generally)
http://www.anderson.ucla.edu/research/japan/

Kentucky
http://www.kytourism.com/intro.html

Louisiana, New Orleans
http://www.icorp.net/carnival/

Maryland
http://www.mdisfun.org/

Massachusetts
http://www.mass-vacation.com/

Mexico
http://www.go2mexico.com/
http://www.mexico.com/
http://www.mexonline.com/lodging.htm
http://www.vallartaonline.com/

National parks (U.S.)
http://www.nps.gov/

New Hampshire
http://www.visitnh.gov/

Safaris
http://www.onsafari.com/

Smoky Mountains
http://www.smokiesonline.com/

Switzerland
http://www.davos.ch/
http://www.geneve-tourisme.ch/

http://www.gstaad.ch/
http://www.stmoritz.ch/
http://www.switzerlandtourism.ch/
http://www.tcs.ch/FrAccueil.jsp
http://www.zermatt.ch/

Virginia
http://www.virginia.org/home.asp?Try=Yes

Dictionaries

http://www.dictionary.com/
http://www.onelook.com/
http://www.yourdictionary.com/

Diving

http://www.aquatrek.com/

Domain registry

http://www.internic.net/

Education

http://www.educationtogo.com/

Digital library for students
http://www.npac.syr.edu/projects/tutorials/index.html

K–12 links
http://www.jumbo.com/

Internet university
http://www.caso.com/home/index.phtml

U.S. Department of Education
http://www.ed.gov/

Virtual University
http://www.vu.org/

Entertainment

Industry information
http://www.hollywood.com/

Tickets
> http://www.ticketmaster.com/

Disney
> http://disney.go.com/park/homepage/today/flash/
> index.html

Filmzone
> http://www.filmzone.com/

MGM
> http://www.mgm.com/

Sony Studios (Columbia, Tristar)
> http://www.sony.com/

Universal Studios
> http://www.universalstudios.com/homepage/

Warner Brothers
> http://www2.warnerbros.com/web/main/index.jsp

Environment

Earthwatch expeditions and trips
> http://www.earthwatch.org/

Endangered Species Program
> http://endangered.fws.gov/

Geographic information
> http://www.usgs.gov/

National Geographic Society
> http://www.nationalgeographic.com/

Hotel information

Deals, rates, brochures
> http://www.180096hotel.com/
> http://www.travelweb.com/

Hotels with online reservations
> http://www.travelweb.com/

Chateaux Hotels (France)
   http://www.relaischateaux.fr/site/us/home

Embassy Suites
   http://www.embassysuites.com/

Hilton Hotels
   http://www.hilton.com/
   http://www.promus.com/

Melia Hotels
   http://www.solmelia.es/cgi-bin/solmelia/home/home?4

Minotel Switzerland
   http://www.minotel.com/minotelPublic/main/
      home.asp?xlanguage=EN

Ritz-Carlton Hotels
   http://www.ritzcarlton.com/html_corp/home/index.asp

Sandals
   http://www.sandals.com/

Shangri-La Hotels
   http://www.shangri-la.com/eng/index.htm

Swiss Hotels
   http://www.swisshotels.ch/index.cfm

Hotel reservation services

Accommodations Express
   http://www.accommodationsexpress.com/

Central Reservations Service
   http://www.reservationservices.com/

Citywide Reservation Services
   http://www.cityres.com/

Expedia
   http://www.expedia.com/daily/home/travelscape.asp

Express Reservations
   http://www.express-res.com/

Hotel Reservations Network
http://www.180096hotel.com/

Quikbook
http://www.quikbook.com/

RMC Travel Centre
http://www.rmcwebtravel.com/

Immunizations
http://www.tripprep.com/

Internet information
http://infoseek.go.com/

Browsers
http://www.microsoft.com/windows/ie/default.asp
http://browsers.netscape.com/browsers/main.tmpl

History
http://www.zakon.org/robert/internet/timeline/

ISPs
http://www.thelist.com/

Web page design
http://www.webwave.net/
http://whyfiles.org/welcome/write_for_web.html

articles and information
http://hotwired.lycos.com/webmonkey/

backgrounds and graphics
http://home.netscape.com/home/bg/index.html
http://www.iconbazaar.com/main/index.html

bad design
http://www.webpagesthatsuck.com/

The Internet Research Guide
http://cyberatlas.internet.com/

WWW information
http://www.webreference.com/

Languages and translation
http://babelfish.altavista.com/
http://travlang.com/languages/

Maps

CNN's Travel Guide
http://www.cnn.com/TRAVEL/

DeLorme Publishing
http://www.delorme.com/

Lucent Technologies
http://www.mapsonus.com/

MapQuest
http://www.mapquest.com/

Vicinity Corp.
http://www.mapblast.com/myblast/index.mb

Money

Bank rate Monitor Infobank
http://www.bankrate.com/brm/default.asp

Foreign currency conversion
http://www.xe.com/ucc/

Museums

Louvre (Paris)
http://www.louvre.fr/louvrea.htm

Museum of Modern Art (New York City)
http://moma.org/

National Gallery (Washington, D.C.)
http://nga.gov/

News

Links to newspapers
http://www.pcanswer.com/news.htm
http://newslink.org

Personalized
http://my.yahoo.com/p/d.html?v
http://netangels.com/
http://search411.com/

BBC
http://www.bbc.co.uk/?ok

CNN
http://www.cnn.com/

Forbes Digital Tool
http://www.forbes.com/

National Public Radio
http://www.npr.org/

New York Times
http://www.nytimes.com/

Reuters
http://www.reuters.com/news.jhtml

USA Today
http://www.usatoday.com/

Wall Street Journal (interactive edition)
http://online.wsj.com/public/us

News groups (searches)
http://groups.google.com/

Rail

Amtrak
http://amtrak.com/

Europe
   http://www.raileurope.com/us/

Restaurants
   http://eat.epicurious.com/restaurant/
   http://www.menusonline.com/

Search engines
   http://www.search.com/

Commercial sites
   http://www.allbusiness.com/directory/index.jsp

Digital Corp.
   http://altavista.com/

Hotbot
   http://hotbot.lycos.com

Lycos
   http://lycos.cs.cmu.edu/

WebCrawler
   http://www.webcrawler.com/info.wbcrwl/

Yahoo!
   http://www.yahoo.com/

Meta search engines
   http://www.dogpile.com/index.gsp
   http://www.google.com/
   http://www.overture.com/

Telephone directories
   http://www.switchboard.com/

Tours and tour companies

Abercrombie & Kent
   http://www.abercrombiekent.com/

ATA Vacations
   http://www.ata.com/

Caribbean Yacht Charters
http://www.caribbeanyachtcharters.com/

Central Holidays
http://www.centralh.com/

China Travel Service
http://www.chinatravelservice.com/

CIE Tours
http://www.cietours.com/

Collette Tours
http://www.collettevacations.com/

Contiki
http://www.contiki.com/

Continental Airlines Vacations
http://www.coolvacations.com/

Daman Nelson Travel
http://www.daman-nelson.com/

Destination Europe Resources
http://www.der.com/

Far & Wide
http://www.farandwide.com/about_family.html

Funjet Vacations
http://www.funjet.com/index.asp

Globe Tours
http://www.globetours.com/

Haddon Holidays (Hawaii)
http://www.hawaiihoneymoon.com/

Holland American Line Westours
http://www.hollandamerica.com/

INTRAV
http://www.intrav.com/

IsramWorld
http://www.isram.com/index.htm

Kuoni Tours
http://kuoni.ch/

Japan Travel Bureau
http://www.jtbusa.com/

Mountain Vacations
http://www.mountainvacations.com/

Northwest WorldVacations
http://www.nwa.com/travel/

Pleasant Holidays
http://www.pleasantholidays.com/index.jsp

Southwest Airlines Fun Pack Vacations
http://www.swavacations.com/

Special Expeditions (Lindblad)
http://www.specialexpeditions.com/

Sunburst Holidays
http://www.sunburstholidays.com/

Sunny Land Tours
http://www.sunnylandtours.com/

United Vacations
http://www.unitedvacations.com/

Worry-Free Vacations (MLT Vacations)
http://www.worryfreevacations.com/
wf_hmIndex?aid=dsp

Travel agencies online

All-World Travel
http://www.awtravel.com/

American Express
http://travel.americanexpress.com/travel

Biztravel
http://www.biztravel.com/

Compass Travel
http://www.compasstravel.com/cruises.htm

Internet Travel Network
http://www.itn.net/cgi/get?itn/pl/amex_personal/index

Microsoft Expedia
http://www.expedia.com/Default.asp

PCTravel
http://www.pctravel.com/

Rosenbluth International
http://www.rosenbluth.com/content/home/home.htm

Sato Travel
http://www.satotravel.com/

Space Adventures
http://www.spaceadventures.com/

TENonline Services
http://www.tenonline.com/

Traveler's Net
http://travelersnet.com/

Travelocity
http://www.travelocity.com

Travel Associates, Inc.
http://www.tvlassoc.com/

Travelweb
http://travelweb.com/

World Travel Partners
http://www.worldtravel.com/wtbti/index.asp

Travel bargains and deals
http://www.bestfares.com/home.asp

http://www.lowestfare.com/cgi-bin/gx.cgi/
AppLogic+lowestfare.home.Home
http://www.travelersnet.com/
http://www.discounttravel.com/
http://www.etn.nl/

Budget travel

http://www.greentortoise.com/

Travel guides

http://www.atevo.com/
http://www.fodors.com/
http://www.travel-library.com/
http://www.wtgonline.com/navigate/world.asp

Travel information (general)

http://www.cheaptripsonline.com/
http://www.lonelyplanet.com/
http://www.travel-library.com/
http://www.vacations.com/
http://www.virtualtourist.com

Business travelers

http://www.trip.com/trs/trip/home/index_01.xsl

TravelTrade publications

http://www.traveltrade.com/index.jsp

Travel Weekly

http://www.traveler.net/updates

United States Government

Statistics

http://www.fedstats.gov/

Travelers' health

http://www.cdc.gov/travel/

Census Bureau

http://www.census.gov/

Federal Aviation Administration
http://www.faa.gov/

Fish and Wildlife Service
http://www.fws.gov/

International Trade Administration
http://ita.doc.gov/

Small Business Administration
http://www.sba.gov/

State Department
http://www.state.gov/

Trade and Development Agency
http://www.tda.gov/

Weather
http://www.weather.com/

Appendix B

Tell the World about Your Site

■ Free Sites

At some of these sites you simply register. At others, you may want to submit a brief summary of what makes your page interesting and unique.

BizWeb
> http://www.bizweb.com/

CADvision
> http://home.cadvision.com/accounts/home/

Galaxy
> http://www.galaxy.com/

Internet Mall
> http://www.internet.com/sections/lists.html

Internic: *Write to*
> admin@ds.internic.net

Lycos
> http://searchservices.lycos.com/searchservices/

Netscape
> http://home.mcom.com/home/whats-new.html

WebCrawler
> http://web.webcrawler.com/d/search/p/webcrawler/

Yahoo
> http://docs.yahoo.com/info/suggest/

Appendix C

Host Types and Countries of Origin

Each URL ends with a two- to five-letter suffix indicating what kind of organization the URL belongs to (in the United States), or in which country other than the United States the URL is located.

■ Suffixes Used in the United States (Top Level Domains)

Arts and entertainment	.arts
Commercial	.com
Universities and colleges	.edu
Businesses and firms	.biz
Government	.gov
Providers of information services	.info
Military	.mil
ISPs, networks	.net
Personal or individual	.name
Organizations	.org
Recreation and entertainment	.rec
Business offering goods for sale	.store
Activities relating to the Web	.web

■ Suffixes Indicating Countries Other than the United States

Antigua and Barbuda	.ag
Argentina	.ar
Australia	.au
Austria	.at
Bahrain	.bh
Belgium	.be

Belize	.bz
Bermuda	.bm
Brazil	.br
Brunei Darussalam	.bn
Bulgaria	.bg
Cambodia	.kh
Canada	.ca
Chile	.cl
China	.cn
Cook Islands	.ck
Costa Rica	.cr
Croatia	.hr
Czech Republic	.cz
Denmark	.dk
Dominican Republic	.do
Ecuador	.ec
Egypt	.eg
Estonia	.ee
Finland	.fi
France	.fr
Germany	.de
Gibraltar	.gi
Great Britain	.gb
Greece	.gr
Guatemala	.gt
Hong Kong	.hk
Hungary	.hu
Iceland	.ic
India	.in
Iran	.ir
Ireland	.ie
Israel	.il
Italy	.it
Jamaica	.jm
Japan	.jp

Kuwait	.kw
Latvia	.lv
Lithuania	.lt
Macau	.mo
Macedonia	.mk
Malaysia	.my
Malta	.mt
Mauritius	.mu
Mexico	.mx
Mozambique	.mz
Namibia	.na
Netherlands	.nl
New Zealand	.nz
Norway	.no
Pakistan	.pk
Peru	.pe
Philippines	.ph
Poland	.pl
Portugal	.pt
Romania	.ro
Russia	.ru/.su
Saint Lucia	.lc
Saudi Arabia	.sa
Singapore	.sg
Slovak Republic	.sk
South Africa	.za
South Korea	.kr
Spain	.es
Sri Lanka	.lk
Sweden	.se
Switzerland	.ch
Taiwan	.tw
Thailand	.th
Trinidad and Tobago	.tt
Turkey	.tr

Ukraine	.ua
United Arab Emirates	.ae
United Kingdom	.uk
United States of America	.us
[U.S. outlying islands	.um]
Uruguay	.uy
Uzbekistan	.uz
Venezuela	.ve
Vietnam	.vn
Zambia	.zm
Zimbabwe	.zw

Glossary

Apple A computer company whose brands and models include the Macintosh, PowerBook, and iMac. The Apple operating system is different from the DOS and Windows systems.

applet A self-contained program that is downloaded to your computer through your browser; once downloaded, it does its job, such as creating animated and interactive features.

ARPAnet A network of computers established in the 1960s by the U.S. Department of Defense Advanced Research Projects Agency (ARPA, renamed DARPA in the 1970s). ARPAnet's purpose was to enable the exchange of information among universities and scientific and research organizations; the military also used this network for communication.

bandwidth The amount of data that can be transmitted through a particular medium, such as a telephone line, cable television cable, or wireless communication device. *See also* bps.

bps Bits per second, used to express modem transmission speed.

browser The software (application) that acts as the tool for accessing the Internet and determines how a Web page is displayed on a screen. The most-used Web browsers are Microsoft Internet Explorer and Netscape.

cable modem High-speed modem that connects a computer to the Internet via cable television wire and fiber-optic connections. The latter carry much more information than conventional copper wire and are far less subject to electromagnetic interference.

CATV Cable television.

CD-ROM drive A drive that allows your computer to access the information or programs stored on a compact disc (CD).

CGI Script A common gateway interface program that gives instructions to your server. Such scripts are necessary for complex processing of some Web pages.

commission caps Absolute dollar limits on commissions paid by airlines to travel agencies and agents.

computer graphics Applications that allow the user to create graphic works such as drawings, maps, special titles, animations, and the like.

computerized reservation system (CRS) Proprietary reservation systems such as Amadeus, Apollo, SABRE, and Worldspan.

connectivity The ability to work or communicate with diverse computer equipment types. *See also* protocol.

CRS *See* computerized reservation system.

cyber- Prefix denoting the computer- and/or electronic-relatedness of the modified word. New words and phrases beginning with *cyber* are coined daily. They all go back to *cybernetics,* the theoretical study of communication and control processes in biological, mechanical, and electronic systems, especially the comparison of these processes in biological and artificial systems.

cyber literacy The ability and skill to use online services effectively.

cyberspace The universe of the Internet, in which persons interact by means of connected computers. A defining characteristic of cyberspace is that communication is independent of physical distance.

database Any stored collection of data that can be manipulated.

database management The creation and manipulation of a set of interrelated files that may include data, text, spreadsheet, graphic, audio, and video content. An interactive database, ideally, seamlessly integrates all these file types into a comprehensive and user-friendly information system.

desktop publishing The use of a personal computer to produce high-quality electronic and printed output that is ready for the printer or marked up for use as a Web page.

DOS (Disk Operating System) Computer operating system software developed by Microsoft.

download To move information from a distant computer to one's own computer.

Dynamic HTML (DHTML) A newer version of HTML that works only on Netscape 4.0 and MS Explorer 4.0 and higher. Older browsers do not recognize DHTML.

e-commerce Electronic commerce; typically, sales conducted via the Internet.

e-mail The transmission of messages over a network. Users can send e-mail to a single recipient or broadcast the same message to multiple users. Attachments can be used to transmit large files in addition to the e-mail message.

Explorer *See* Internet Explorer.

Federal Aviation Administration (FAA) The agency of the U.S. government with primary responsibility for the safety of civil aviation.

FAT (File Allocation Table) Application that partitions a computer's hard disk.

Frame relay A packet-switching protocol for use on wide-area networks. Frame relay transmits variable-length packets at up to 1.544 Mbps.

FTP (File Transfer Protocol) A technique to transfer files from one computer to another.

GIF (Graphics Information File) A file suffix describing a common Web graphic format.

giga One billion (one gigabyte = one billion bytes).

Global Distribution System (GDS) Another term for CRS.

GUI (Graphical User Interface) An onscreen environment that uses icons, menus, and dialog boxes to represent programs, files, and options; each graphic item can be activated by pointing and clicking with a mouse.

hard disk (hard drive) A personal computer's main data storage space; the bigger the better.

HDTV (high-definition television) A type of television that has twice as many lines on the screen as traditional sets; data is used in digital form.

hit A visit to a Web site, as recorded in the log of the site's Web server. A visit to an HTML page containing three graphic images results in four hits in the log.

home-based agents Travel agents using the home as their main base of operations.

home page The first page of a multipage Web site.

HTML (HyperText Markup Language) A set of special codes (*tags*) that are embedded in the text of a Web page to add formatting and linking information. Typical format information includes line and paragraph breaks; typical linking information allows users to point and click to move to different parts of the same Web page, to other pages on the same Web site, or to altogether different Web sites.

HTTP (HyperText Transfer Protocol) The set of rules regulating the transfer of Web-formatted data.

hypertext The main idea of the World Wide Web; the ability to jump from link to link by pointing and clicking.

Internet A worldwide network of computers that enables the exchange of information in a variety of formats.

Internet Explorer (Microsoft) A proprietary browser developed by Microsoft.

Internet service provider (ISP) An organization or company that offers Internet/Web access to end users.

Java A compiled computer code created by Sun Microsystems especially for use on the World Wide Web.

Javascript A language used in Web design to create mouse rollovers and other special effects.

JPEG/JPG (Joint Photographic Experts Group) A file format/suffix denoting a common Web graphic format; usually used for photographs.

LAN (local area network) A limited network of linked computers such as within an agency, company, or school. Now mostly synonymous with *intranet*.

laptop A portable computer that can be used, literally, on one's lap.

Linux An operating system invented by Linus Torvalds at the University of Helsinki in Finland. This system is very complete, fast, and free; both the system and its source code are openly available.

Macintosh A brand and model of Apple Computer.

mainframe Large computer, often the hub of a vast network with many users; an example is a CRS.

microprocessor A complex chip that is the central processing unit (CPU) of a personal computer. All the computer's operations are controlled from and accomplished here.

Microsoft (MS) A Seattle-based software company headed by Bill Gates; its products include the Windows systems, Internet Explorer, FrontPage, Works, Office, and many other programs.

MIME (Multipurpose Internet Mail Extension) An addition to the original e-mail protocol that allows the exchange of audio, graphic, and video information in addition to the basic ASCII files.

minicomputer A stand-alone enterprise machine sized between the personal computer and the mainframe computer; few if any of these are produced now.

Modem (MOdulation-DEModulation) Hardware that adapts a terminal or computer to a CATV or telephone line for the transmission of data.

mouse The device needed to point and click.

MS *See* Microsoft.

NASDAQ (National Association of Securities Dealers Automated Quotation) system A virtual stock exchange that lists the stock of many publicly traded companies.

Netscape A company that produces popular Internet browsers, including Netscape Communicator and Netscape Navigator.

niche marketing Marketing to a small, distinct group of people.

operating system (OS) The main system of a computer that manages and enables all other programs/applications.

personal computer (PC) A small desktop or laptop computer; usually denotes an IBM-compatible machine.

personalized news service Online service that continually scans the Internet for information in accordance with your instructions.

platform The underlying computer operating system on which application programs can run, such as Windows.

point and click An essential and basic activity, accomplished with the mouse, in Apple and Windows environments.

presentation software An application that enables the creation of high-quality documents or Web pages; contents may include pictures, text, and other elements.

programming language An artificial language (set of codes and rules) used to give instructions to a computer.

protocol A set of rules or "language" that enables computers to "talk" to each other, thereby enabling connectivity (*see* connectivity).

psychographic traits Personality characteristics of a group; often used in connection with marketing surveys that also measure demographic traits.

random access memory (RAM) The personal computer's working memory, which is active only when the computer is turned on.

read only memory (ROM) A storage chip containing hardwired instructions to boot up the computer.

search engine A means of locating information on the Internet.

server An online computer that stores Web site information and sends it to users over the Internet.

site Usually refers to an entire Web site rather than a single Web page (*see* Web site).

SOHO Acronym for "small office/home office"; a home-based travel agent might be considered SOHO.

spreadsheet Software that simulates a paper spreadsheet or worksheet in which columns of numbers are summed or calculated; typically used for budgets and planning.

TCP/IP (Transmission Control Protocol/Internet Protocol) The standard for data transmission over networks, including the Internet, intranets, and extranets.

telephony Use of a computer to make phone calls via the Internet.

ticketless travel Ticketing technique that allows passengers to board a plane without a paper ticket. All relevant information is stored and transmitted electronically.

touchpad An alternative point-and-click device.

URL (Uniform Resource Locator) An Internet address.

upload To move information from one's own computer to a distant computer.

Usenet An older area on the Internet that allows text-only access to discussion groups; the discussion groups may be organized by specific topic, such as travel to a particular area, city, or country.

videoconferencing At its simplest, a technique that allows people both to talk to each other and see each other via the Internet. More sophisticated equipment gives small groups of people the opportunity to virtually meet with each other.

Web page One page of a Web site.

Web site A collection of Web pages. Although each page is referred to as a *Web page,* the first page is called the *home page* or *index page.*

Windows Microsoft's proprietary operating system.

World Wide Web The most popular area of the Internet, which allows the easy exchange and transmission of text, graphics, audio, and video.

Word processing The creation and management of (primarily) text documents.

XML (Extensible Markup Language) An improved version of HTML.

Index